THE ENCYCLOPEDIA OF
Knitting Techniques

MELANIE PORTER
JAMES VINTAGE 'EGG' CHAIR

THE ENCYCLOPEDIA OF
Knitting Techniques

Lesley Stanfield and Melody Griffiths

Search Press

A QUARTO BOOK

This edition published in 2018 by
Search Press
Wellwood
North Farm Road
Tunbridge Wells
Kent TN2 3DR

Previously published as
The Encyclopedia of Knitting Techniques
in 2000 and as *The New Encyclopedia
of Knitting Techniques* in 2011

ISBN: 978-1-78221-644-5

Conceived, edited and designed by
Quarto Publishing
an imprint of The Quarto Group
The Old Brewery
6 Blundell Street
London N7 9BH
www.quartoknows.com

QUAR: EKTN

Editor & designer: Michelle Pickering
Picture researcher: Susannah Jayes
Editorial assistant: Cassie Lawrence
Publisher: Samantha Warrington

Printed in China

Contents

STITCH COLLECTION 50

DESIGN AND INSPIRATION 132

Introduction

Knitting is the art of constructing a flexible fabric from a notionally continuous thread. The surface of the fabric can be smooth or textured, and the knitted pieces can be flat or tubular, straight or shaped, in infinite variety.

Chapter One contains all the essential information you need to get started, from the basic skills of how to work knit and purl stitches to techniques for shaping and embellishing your knitting.

Chapter Two features a collection of more than 150 traditional and original stitch patterns – explore, experiment and adapt them to create knitting that is all your own work.

Chapter Three features practical advice for creating your own designs, plus examples of finished pieces from knitwear designers as inspiration to get you started.

◀ JENNIFER TARAN
BEACH DAY SHAWL
Knitted in four colours and four different stitch patterns, this lacy shawl showcases the wonderful textures and patterns that can be created with simple stitches and techniques. The sections of the shawl represent ocean waves, marram grass on sand dunes, summer skies and sunshine. The shawl can be wrapped around the shoulders, worn as a cowl or buttoned like a sleeveless sweater.

Knitting Skills

There is very little you need to know about knitting to get started – knit and purl are the only two stitches to learn. It is then simply a case of combining them in different ways to produce different effects. This chapter features practical guidance and step-by-step instruction for a wide range of knitting techniques.

Using medium-size needles and a smooth, medium-weight pure wool yarn, practise the steps on the following pages for casting on, knit and purl, and casting off and soon you will be knitting smoothly and rhythmically. You will then learn how to read patterns and charts and work simple shaping so that you can use your newfound knitting skills to make something.

Once you have mastered the basics of knitting, you can begin to explore some of the additional techniques for creating special effects. Finally, you will find guidance on choosing appropriate finishing techniques, which can make all the difference to the success of your project.

◄ JENNIFER TARAN
I-CORD BABY PANTS
Made in soft lambswool, these baby pants are knitted in the round in stocking stitch with ribbed cuffs and eyelets around the waistband for the I-cord drawstring – simple, cute and cosy.

Equipment

You do not need complicated or expensive equipment to learn to knit – just knitting needles and yarn. As you progress in the craft, you can collect more equipment as you need it.

To experiment with different yarns and tensions, you will need knitting needles in different sizes. You will also need a cable needle for working cable stitch patterns, and double-pointed needles or a circular needle if you want to try knitting in the round.

When you are ready to knit a garment, you will need a tape measure or ruler, stitch holders, scissors, a tapestry or yarn needle, and maybe a few other items of equipment.

Knitting needles

Knitting needles are an investment because you will use them time and time again. Look after your needles carefully and they will last for years, but when the points are damaged or the needles are bent, it is time to throw them out and buy new ones.

Straight knitting needles

Pairs of needles are made in a variety of lengths, ranging from around 25cm (10in) to 40cm (16in). Most knitting needles are aluminium, usually with a pearl-grey finish, though some are nickel-plated. Larger needles are made of plastic to reduce their weight. Bamboo needles are a flexible alternative.

Circular needles

Circular needles are simply two short needle ends joined by a flexible nylon or plastic cord. The length of a circular needle is measured from needle tip to needle tip. Most sizes are in lengths of 40cm (16in) to 120cm (47in).

Double-pointed needles

Double-pointed needles are sold in sets of four or five, and in several lengths. They were traditionally made of steel, but aluminium needles are more usual now, with bamboo and plastic in some sizes.

Cable needles

These are used for knitting cable stitch patterns. Some have a kink or crank to help keep the stitches on the needle.

Other equipment

Scissors, a tape measure and sewing needles are essential items, but you will also find some other knitter's notions useful or even indispensable.

Sewing needles

You will need blunt-pointed needles – either tapestry or yarn needles – in different sizes for different weights of yarn.

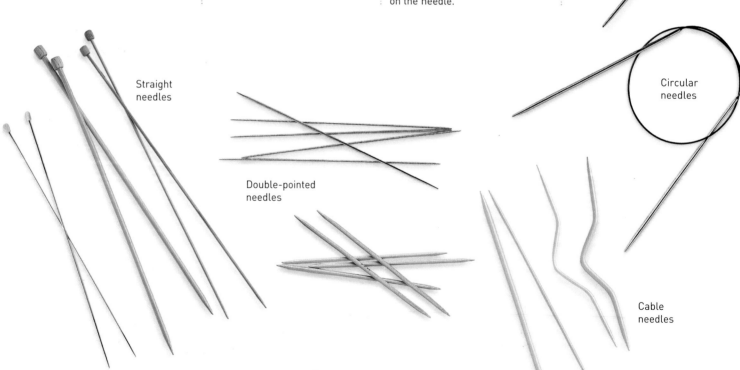

Sewing needles

Straight needles

Double-pointed needles

Circular needles

Cable needles

Scissors

Choose scissors that are not too small and not too large, but very sharp.

Tape measure

The most useful tape measures have centimetres and inches on the same side, so that you can compare measurements.

Row counter

A row counter helps you to keep your place.

Point protectors

Little point protectors stop the stitches from falling off the needles if you have to leave your knitting in the middle of a row.

Needle gauge

A knitting needle gauge with metric and imperial sizes (often one on each side) can be useful.

Bobbins

Bobbins are used to prevent multiple lengths of yarn from tangling together during intarsia colour knitting.

Knitter's thimble

Worn on the index finger of the hand that holds the yarn, this is used for managing multiple lengths of yarn in stranded colour knitting.

Crochet hook

A crochet hook can be used to rescue dropped stitches as well as to cast off.

Finally, for fun

Though not strictly necessary, pompom rings and a knitting bobbin are great for getting children interested in handling yarn; they also make short work of creating decorative extras.

Point protectors

Crochet hooks

Scissors

Row counters

Bobbins

Pompom rings

Needle gauge

Tape measure

Knitter's thimble

Knitting bobbin

Yarns

Feeling the yarn as it slips through your fingers is one of the pleasures of knitting. Add to that enjoyment by exploring a whole range of yarns, from fine and smooth to chunky and textured, in synthetic blends and natural fibres.

Yarn is presented either as a ready-wound ball or a wind-it-yourself hank. The fibre content and construction determine how much yarn you get for the weight, so two balls that weigh the same may be very different sizes or contain very different lengths of yarn. Whatever you choose, buy the best you can afford and your knitting will last.

Smooth yarns

Sometimes called classic yarns, these smooth yarns in wool, cotton or mixed fibres are the knitter's reliable friends. However fine or thick these yarns are, they will always show up stitch patterns beautifully.

Textured yarns

Fibres such as alpaca, silk and linen make yarns that look smooth in the ball but have a distinct character when knitted. Mohair and angora can be used alone or mixed with other fibres for a soft and fluffy surface. Flecked and marled yarns give a tweedy effect, while roving yarns are single-ply and loosely twisted, giving a handspun look.

Wool and cotton yarn

Cotton yarn

Lambswool and alpaca yarn

Alpaca yarn

Bamboo yarn

Mohair and silk yarn

Wool and cotton yarn

Merino wool yarn

Handspun tweed yarn

Novelty yarns

Also called fashion yarns, these change from season to season — one year tweedy bouclés fill the shops; next time you look everything is metallic. Chenille's velvety texture is a perennial favourite, but it is worth trying them all — from shiny ribbon yarns to richly textured blends.

> **KNITTING WITH RIBBON TRIM**
>
> It is possible to knit with ribbon trim, but ribbon yarns tend to be more flexible and easier to knit with than the ribbon you would use as trim. Ribbon trim may not be very hard-wearing or launder well, and it is also more expensive than ribbon yarn.

Speciality yarns

Some yarns are designed for a specific purpose, such as for knitting socks. Sock yarns are often fine-weight, and they may have elastin, nylon or both added to produce socks with a snug fit. Self-striping and hand-dyed yarns are particularly popular for knitting socks.

Improvised yarns

Experiment with string or raffia; rip strips of cotton fabric and join them with knots; or cut spirals from cloth, plastic sheeting or mock leather or suede, and sew the ends together. If you can make a continuous thread out of it, you can knit with it.

Fur-effect yarn

Eyelash yarn

Ribbon yarn

Self-striping sock yarn

Yarn from recycled fabric

Raffia and string

Bouclé yarn

Multicoloured yarn

Cord

Holding Yarn and Needles

Knitting is a two-handed craft in which stitches are worked off the left needle and on to the right. To get started, sit comfortably and relax. Knitting requires hand and eye coordination, which is hard to achieve if you are tense.

There are many ways to hold and control the yarn and needles, and there is no single correct method. Experiment with those suggested here until you find one that suits you.

Holding the yarn

The yarn runs through and around the fingers, leaving the fingertips free to manipulate the needles and control the yarn. The holds shown here have been devised in order to feed the yarn on to the needle evenly. In each of the holds, the working end of the yarn that feeds on to the needle is over the index finger; the ball of yarn feeds on to the little finger.

Loosely in right hand
To tension the yarn loosely, simply slip the yarn alternately over and under the fingers.

More firmly in right hand
To tension the yarn more firmly, wrap the yarn around the little finger, then over and under the other fingers.

Loosely in left hand
To tension the yarn loosely, try taking it over the little finger, under the next two and around the index finger.

More firmly in left hand
To tension the yarn more firmly, wrap the yarn around the little finger, then under and over the other fingers.

Holding the needles

Once you are holding the yarn, pick up a pair of needles, one in each hand, and try out these different holds. Some knitters hold the right needle like a pen; others hold it overhand like a knife. The left needle is usually held overhand. With the free-needle (or pen) hold, the needles used are as short as is practical, and the weight of the knitting on the right needle is supported by the hand and wrist. With the fixed-needle (or knife) hold, long needles are used, and the right needle is tucked under the arm for support.

Fixed needle with yarn in right hand

With your right hand, pick up a needle, hold it overhand like a knife and tuck the end of the needle under your arm. Take the other needle in your left hand, holding it lightly over the top. Practise moving the left needle against the right. When knitting, you will find that you can let go of the right needle each time you make a stitch.

Free needle with yarn in right hand

With your right hand, pick up a needle and hold it like a pen. Take the other needle in your left hand, holding it lightly over the top. Try moving the needles forwards and back with your fingertips, keeping your elbows relaxed at your sides. When you cast on and start knitting, do not drop the right needle to manipulate the yarn; instead, support it in the crook of your t humb and use your index finger to control the yarn.

Yarn in left hand

Hold the needle in your right hand like a pen or knife as preferred; hold the needle in your left hand lightly over the top. When knitting, hold the yarn taut with the left hand while hooking or catching it with the point of the right needle.

Basic Cast-ons

The first step in beginning any piece of knitting is to cast on some stitches. Here are three of the most useful ways to cast on.

The two-needle cable cast-on makes a strong edge with a rope-like twist, but it is not very elastic. The thumb cast-on uses just one needle and is versatile. It is very compatible with ribs due to its elasticity. Used with garter stitch, it is indistinguishable from the rest of the knitting because it is, in effect, a knit row. The backward loop cast-on also uses one needle; it is simple and useful for buttonholes.

TIPS

Cable cast-on: A less robust cable cast-on is made if you take the needle into the stitch each time, instead of between stitches. This creates a useful edge for hems.

Thumb cast-on: Measuring out three times the length of the cast-on edge for the thumb cast-on can be cumbersome when you require a large number of stitches. An alternative method is to use a slip knot to join together the ends from two balls of yarn, then hold one strand with the left hand and the other with the right hand and work the cast-on. Once the required number of stitches has been cast on, discard the yarn in the left hand and continue working with the yarn in the right.

Provisional cast-on: The thumb cast-on can also be used to create a provisional cast-on. A length of smooth contrast yarn is used in the left hand. This is then unpicked and the loose stitch loops are picked up and worked in the other direction.

Slip knot

Putting a slip knot on the needle makes your first stitch. You can coil the yarn around your fingers or lay it flat.

1 Coil the yarn into a loop, then bring the strand forwards and through the loop. Insert the needle as shown to secure the yarn.

2 Pull one end to tighten the knot, then gently pull the other end of the yarn to close the knot up to the needle. You are now ready to cast on.

Cable cast-on

This cast-on is made by knitting a stitch, then transferring it from the right to the left needle.

1 Leaving a short end, make a slip knot on one needle. Holding this needle in the left hand, insert the other needle into the front of the slip knot. Take the yarn around the right needle and pull through a stitch, then transfer it to the left needle.

2 From now on, insert the right needle between the stitches each time. Transfer each new stitch to the left needle as before.

Thumb cast-on

Also known as long-tail cast-on, this method involves simply knitting each stitch off your thumb.

Backward loop cast-on

Tension the yarn carefully for this cast-on, which is often used at the end of rows.

1 Measure off about three times the length of the edge to be cast on and make a slip knot on the needle. Hold the needle and yarn from the ball in your right hand.

3 Take the yarn around the needle, then draw a loop through to make a stitch. Gently pull the end to close the stitch up to the needle. Repeat until the required number of stitches, including the slip knot, have been cast on.

2 Tensioning the other end of the yarn in your left hand, make a loop around your thumb and insert the right needle into the loop.

Leaving a short end, make a slip knot on the needle. Tension the yarn in your left hand, and make a loop around your thumb. Insert the needle in the loop, slip your thumb out and gently pull the yarn to make a stitch on the needle.

More Cast-ons

These three cast-ons are not necessarily more difficult than the basic cast-on methods, but they will expand your repertoire of techniques to give you more options in your knitting. Once you are familiar with different cast-ons, you can decide whether to substitute one for another to achieve a particular result.

SEE ALSO
• Basic cast-ons, pages 16–17

Selecting a cast-on

The cast-on method you choose depends upon the finished outcome you require – an elastic or firm cast-on, decorative or plain. In some cases, an extra-strong cast-on may be required, such as on children's garments where edges may be prone to hard wear. Interesting cast-on or cast-off edges can also transform a simple garment.

For example, the Channel Island cast-on is both strong and decorative, and can look especially good on the edge of collars and cuffs.

The basic skills will take you a long way in knitting, but sometimes the more unusual techniques can make all the difference to the success of your garments. Learning how and when to use alternative techniques is the first step towards designing for yourself.

Channel island cast-on

Strongly defined knots decorate the edge of this robust cast-on. For an odd number of stitches, work as described here. For an even number of stitches, simply cast on one more stitch at the end.

Leaving an end six times the length of the edge to be cast on, put a slip knot on one needle. Double this length back on itself so that the free end hangs down where it meets the needle at the slip knot. Take the doubled end in your left hand and the single strand from the ball in your right hand.

Wind the doubled end twice around the thumb of your left hand. Insert the needle up through both of the double strands of yarn on your thumb, then take the single strand around the needle and pull through a stitch. Drop the double strands off the thumb and pull on the ends to bring the knot up to the needle. Bring the single strand forwards and then over the needle to make a second stitch. Continue to make pairs of stitches in this way, ending with a stitch knitted from the thumb.

Channel Island cast-on
The decorative quality of this cast-on can be seen on the lower edge of a typical Guernsey sweater.

Right-slanting single decreases

The two decreases below create a slope to the right on the knit side of the fabric.

Knit two stitches together (k2 tog)

Knitting two stitches together on a knit row makes a smooth shaping, with the second stitch lying on top of the first.

1 Insert the right needle through the front of the first two stitches on the left needle, then take the yarn around the needle.

2 Draw the loop through and drop the two stitches off the left needle.

Purl two stitches together (p2 tog)

For a decrease worked on a purl row that slants to the right on the knit side of the fabric, purl two stitches together.

Left-slanting single decreases

The following four decreases create a slope to the left on the knit side of the fabric.

Slip-knit-pass slipped stitch over (skpo)

Worked on a knit row, this method creates a slope to the left, with the first stitch lying on top of the second.

1 Insert the right needle knitwise through the front of the first stitch on the left needle, and slip it on to the right. Knit the next stitch.

2 Use the tip of the left needle to lift the slipped stitch over the knitted stitch and drop it off the right needle.

Slip-slip-knit (ssk)

This is another popular left-slanting single decrease that is worked on a knit row, although it often causes some confusion. Work to the position of the decrease, insert the right needle knitwise through the front of the first stitch on the left needle and slip it on to the right needle. Repeat this with the next stitch on the left needle, then insert the left needle through both slipped stitches from left to right so that the left needle is in front of the right needle. Knit the two stitches together. This produces a very neat decrease that looks like a left-slanting version of knit two stitches together.

Purl two stitches together through back of loops (p2 tog tbl)

For a decrease worked on a purl row that slants to the left on the knit side of the fabric, purl two stitches together through the back of the loops.

Slip-slip-purl (ssp)

This single decrease is also worked on a purl row to create a slope to the left on the knit side of the fabric. Work to the position of the decrease, insert the right needle knitwise through the front of the first stitch on the left needle and slip it on to the right. Repeat this with the next stitch on the left needle. Slip the stitches back on to the left needle without twisting them again. Then, using the right needle, purl the two stitches together through the back of the loops.

Double Decreases

Sometimes it is necessary to decrease several stitches together rather than work a series of single decreases.

A double decrease shapes the knitting more rapidly. In single rib, a double decrease can be placed so that the pattern is not interrupted on the following row. In many stitch patterns, double decreases are used with double increases to create beautiful lacy effects.

All decreases can be adapted to make multiple decreases by taking more stitches together, but it is very important to be aware of the position of the stitch that lies on top. Always pair a left-slanting and a right-slanting decrease when shaping a garment or working a stitch pattern. The dominant centre stitch of the centred double decrease makes a design feature of shaped darts and gives a clean line to lace patterns.

Right-slanting double decreases
The two decreases below create a slope to the right on the knit side of the fabric.

Knit three stitches together (k3 tog)
Worked on a knit row, the stitch farthest to the left will lie on top, giving a decrease that slants to the right.

Insert the right needle into the front of the third stitch, then through the fronts of the other two stitches. Take the yarn around the needle in the usual way, draw the loop through and drop the three stitches off the left needle.

Purl three stitches together (p3 tog)
For a double decrease worked on a purl row that slants to the right on the knit side of the fabric, purl three stitches together. Insert the right needle into the fronts of the next three stitches, take the yarn around the needle in the usual way, draw the loop through and drop the three stitches off the left needle.

Left-slanting double decreases
The two decreases below create a slope to the left on the knit side of the fabric.

Slip one, knit two together, pass slipped stitch over (sk2po)
Worked on a knit row, the slipped stitch is passed over a single decrease.

Slip the first stitch knitwise, knit the next two stitches together, then lift the first stitch over as shown. The first stitch lies on top, so the decrease slants to the left.

Purl three stitches together through back of loops (p3 tog tbl)
For a double decrease worked on a purl row that slants to the left on the knit side of the fabric, purl three stitches together through the back of the loops.

TIP
Purling several stitches together is a lot easier than knitting them together, so try to finish off large bobbles with a purl stitch.

Balanced decreases at sides
To balance decreases at each side of the fabric, as shown here, work rib 5, then knit 3 together at the beginning of the row. At the end of the row, slip 1, knit 2 together, pass the slipped stitch over, rib 5. The decreases reduce three stitches to one each time, so that the rib pattern remains correct on the following rows.

Picking up Stitches

Centred double decrease

Working a double decrease that takes one stitch from each side and leaves the centre stitch on top has lots of potential for shaping and for working beautiful stitch patterns.

1 Insert the right needle into the second and first stitches as if to knit two together, and slip these stitches on to the right needle.

2 Knit the next stitch, then lift the two slipped stitches over it. The centre stitch of the decrease will lie on top.

Balanced decreases at centre

In this swatch, the ribs travel to the centre and the decreased stitches are neatly hidden under the centre stitch. The rib remains correct for the following rows.

This technique is vital for a well-finished garment because it eliminates bulky seams. Try to make it as neat as possible.

Picking up stitches simply involves knitting up new stitches along an edge, ready to work a band or border in another direction. To pick up a given number of stitches along an edge, fold it in half, mark the halfway point, then fold each half and mark the quarters. Divide the required number of stitches by four, and pick up this number of stitches evenly from each marked quarter.

Picking up along a straight edge

The secret of a satisfactory picked-up edge is to pick up the right number of stitches. When picking up from row ends, do not work into every row end or the band will flare. Skip row ends at regular intervals so that the band will lie flat. To pick up along a cast-on or cast-off edge, work into every stitch.

How to pick up a stitch

For an even finish, use a slightly smaller needle than was used to knit the project previously and pick up stitches at regular intervals.

With the right side facing you, insert the needle under an edge stitch, take the yarn around and pull a loop through to make a stitch. Repeat for each required stitch. Remember that the next row will be a wrong-side row.

Picking up along a shaped edge

Do not skip stitches along the shaped edges of a neckline; work into every decrease and row end. When picking up from a stitch pattern, space stitches as necessary to fit in with the pattern.

Single Increases

increases have two functions. They can be used to increase the number of stitches in a row, such as in chest shaping and top-down yokes, or combined with decreases to create stitch patterns. A single increase adds to the width of the knitting by one stitch at a time.

Balanced single increases

If you work a bar increase into the first stitch in a row, the increase will appear one stitch in, so the edge will be smooth. Make the increase at the end of the row in the last stitch but one, and the bar will also sit one stitch in from the edge.

Lifted-strand increases can be made the same number of stitches in from each edge. Perfectionists will turn the strand in the opposite direction at each end of a row.

Bar increases

This single increase makes a little bar on the knit side of the fabric at the base of the new stitch. This makes it easier to the count rows between rows with shaping.

Knit into front and back of stitch (inc or kf&b)

Knitting into the front and back of a stitch is the most common increase.

1 Knit into the front of the stitch and pull the loop through, but leave the stitch on the left needle.

2 Knit into the back of the stitch on the left needle.

3 Slip the stitch off the left needle, making two stitches on the right needle. Note that the bar of the new stitch lies on the left.

Purl into front and back of stitch (inc or pf&b)

You can also work a bar increase by purling into the front and back of a stitch.

Balanced bar increases

These bar increases have been worked so that they look as if they are three stitches in from each edge. However, because of the nature of the bar increase, there is one more stitch after the increase on the left edge.

Left-slanting lifted-strand increases

Both of the single increases below create a slope to the left on the knit side of the fabric.

Strand or make one left on a knit row (m1 or m1L)

Making a stitch from the strand between the stitches is a very neat way to increase – it is almost invisible. It is also useful for shaping in colour knitting.

Use the left needle to pick up the strand between the stitches on the needles from the front. The right leg of the lifted strand should be at the front of the left needle. Knit into the back of it to make one new stitch.

Strand or make one left on a purl row (m1 or m1L)

For an increase worked on a purl row that slants to the left on the knit side of the fabric, use the left needle to pick up the strand between the stitches on the needles from the back. The right leg of the lifted strand should be at the front of the left needle. Purl into the back of it to make one new stitch.

Right-slanting lifted-strand increases

Both of the single increases below create a slope to the right on the knit side of the fabric.

Strand or make one right on a knit row (m1 or m1R)

This increase has all the advantages of left-slanting lifted-strand increases, but it slants to the right instead. Use the left needle to pick up the strand between the stitches on the needles from the back. The left leg of the lifted strand should be at the front of the left needle. Knit into the front of it to make one new stitch.

Strand or make one right on a purl row (m1 or m1R)

For a decrease worked on the purl row that slants to the right on the knit side of the fabric, use the left needle to pick up the strand between the stitches on the needles from the front. The left leg of the lifted strand should be at the front of the left needle. Purl into the front of it to make one new stitch.

Balanced lifted-strand increases

If you are shaping at the sides of a garment, work lifted-strand increases one or more stitches in from each edge, allowing the same number of stitches before and after the increase. If you are shaping a dart, leave one or more stitches between increases.

▼ JEANETTE TROTMAN
LACY BEADED SCARF
The most common type of increase used in lace patterns such as this scarf is an open increase known as a yarn over. The yarn is simply taken over the needle to form a new stitch, leaving a lace hole beneath. Yarn overs are often paired with a decrease stitch, so that the fabric remains the same width.

Double Increases

Here are two neat ways to increase two stitches at a time rather than work a series of single increases. Double increases are useful for lace stitches and for keeping stitch patterns such as ribs correct while shaping.

Working twice into a yarn over

If your instructions tell you to make two stitches from a double yarn over on the previous row, try this neat way of pairing the made stitches.

Work to the yarn over, then knit into the back of the loop. Drop the second yarn over off the left needle, then pick it up with the left needle as shown, so that it is turned the other way, and knit into the front of it. The two stitches make a neat inverted V shape over the hole.

Lifted-stitch double increase

Working into each side of the stitch on the row below makes an increase that is decorative and useful for keeping patterns such as rib and moss stitch correct when shaping. This increase can be varied by knitting into the back of the lifted stitch or purling into the lifted stitch.

Work to the increase, lift the next stitch from the row below on to the left needle and knit it. Knit the next stitch on the left needle, then lift the stitch previously knitted into back on to the left needle and knit it again.

Double increases
Shaping in single rib looks very decorative when lifted-stitch double increases are used. To keep the rib correct, knit into the lifted stitches to make knit stitches, and purl into the lifted stitches to make purl stitches.

TIP
The lifted-stitch method can also be used to increase just one stitch. If you knit the lifted stitch and then the next stitch, the increased stitch will lie to the right. If you knit the next stitch and then the lifted stitch, the increased stitch will lie to the left.

Bias and Chevron Knitting

Use increases and decreases within the knitted fabric to create bias and chevron effects. If you increase and decrease one stitch at opposite ends on alternate rows so that the stitch count remains constant, the knitted fabric will slant while the direction of the stitches remains vertical – a technique known as bias knitting.

Decreases at the beginning and increases at the end of a row tilt the fabric to the left; increases at the beginning and decreases at the end tilt the fabric to the right. Although often used to make flexible facings, this principle can also be used to shape knitted fabrics of any size. The examples shown here are in stocking stitch – the stripes are simply to emphasise the slant – but textured stitch patterns and colour motifs can also be shaped in this way. The angle of the slant can be varied by spacing the shapings farther apart.

Put left and right bias shapings together to make a chevron fabric with the stitches fanning out from or travelling into the centre. You will need to work a double increase or decrease at the centre, or use single shapings each side of one or more centre stitches. A single chevron can be used to create a knitted fabric of any size, or you can combine upward- and downward-pointing chevrons to make stitch patterns.

SEE ALSO
• **Decreases and increases, pages 28–34**

Chevron knitting
These examples are in stocking stitch with shaping on every right-side row, but you can vary the spacing of the increases and decreases to suit your stitch pattern.

Double increasing in the centre
Increasing at each side of the centre stitch and decreasing at each end of every right-side row makes the stitches fan out from the centre and forms an upward-pointing chevron.

Double decreasing in the centre
Double decreasing at the centre and increasing at each end of every right-side row makes the stitches travel to the centre and forms a downward-pointing chevron.

Bias knitting
To make a flexible bias strip, cast on a few stitches and work the increases and decreases one or two stitches in from each end.

For a slant to the right
Increase one stitch at the beginning and decrease one stitch at the end of each right-side row.

For a slant to the left
Decrease one stitch at the beginning and increase one stitch at the end of each right-side row.

> **TIP**
> Try bias knitting in a stranded colour pattern. The motifs will seem to move to the left or right, depending on the shapings.

Circular Knitting

Working in the round on double-pointed needles was probably the most common method of knitting until the end of the ninteenth century. Today, many knitters are rediscovering the advantages of this technique.

In circular knitting, it is possible for the right side of the work to be always facing. It is actually easier to do almost every type of knitting in the round, including cables and especially stranded colour patterns. For stocking stitch, you just knit every round. Ribs and moss stitches are worked in the same way but on an even number of stitches. For garter stitch, you will need to knit and purl alternate rounds. Working from charts is simple; you just read each row of the chart from right to left, omitting any edge stitches.

Types of needle

Knitting can be worked in the round using double-pointed needles or a circular needle. Double-pointed needles can be bought in sets of four or five needles. Four is the minimum number of needles that can form a round – three needles to hold the stitches and one to knit with. However, you can use as many more double-pointed needles as you need. Circular needles are perfect for knitting larger projects.

In both cases, care should be taken with the first round. Cast on in the usual way, checking that the stitches are not twisted before working the first round. If using double-pointed needles, divide the number of stitches between all but one of the needles.

Using double-pointed needles
To start, bring the first and last needles together and use the spare needle to knit with. Take care to pull firmly on the yarn each time you work the first stitch on a new needle, or you could leave a ladder of loose stitches.

Using a circular needle
To start, use the needle tip in the right hand to work the stitches on the needle in the left hand. Change to a smaller circular needle or a set of double-pointed needles if the number of stitches decreases and the stitches no longer slide easily around the original needle.

Medallion
This medallion is worked in six sections. The increase is a yarn over made at the start of each section, giving a swirled effect.

Turning Rows

Also known as short-row shaping, this technique is used to shape the knitted fabric without casting off stitches until all the shaping is complete. The short rows are made by turning the needles partway through a row, leaving some of the stitches unworked.

Creating a sloped edge

For a steep slant, leave one or two stitches unworked; leave more for a gentler slope. For symmetrical shaping, leave stitches unworked at both ends. For a smooth transition between rows, wrap the yarn around a slipped stitch to anchor it before turning and working back.

Wrapping stitches

1 Knit the number of stitches needed for the short row, bring the yarn forwards, slip the next stitch purlwise, then take the yarn back.

2 Return the slipped stitch to the left needle, ready to turn and work the next short row.

Working wrapped stitches

Once all the short rows have been worked to create the sloped edge, an extra row or two are usually worked into each stitch on the needle. This produces a smoother edge. The loops around the wrapped stitches can either remain untouched, as shown in the photograph below, or the loops can be disguised by working them together with the stitch around which they are wrapped. To do this, work to the first wrapped stitch, insert the right needle under and through the loop, then work together with the next stitch.

Sloped edge

This swatch shows the use of turning rows to make a sloping edge. The stripes help you to see clearly where the yarn is taken around the slipped stitches. The same technique can be used when turning on a purl row.

Beads and Sequins

Knitting beads or sequins into the fabric gives some very exotic results. They can be worked all over the fabric, in a regular pattern or at random.

SEE ALSO
• **Joining in new balls of yarn, page 27**

Threading

The beads or sequins must be threaded on to the yarn before being knitted into the fabric. If possible, buy beads or sequins ready-strung, tie the fine nylon thread to the end of the yarn and slide the beads on to the yarn. Thread an estimated quantity and, when these are used up, break the yarn and thread a fresh quantity. Do this at the end of a row and join in the new yarn in the usual way.

To thread loose beads, take a piece of fine wire about 5cm (2in) long, lay the end of the knitting yarn across it, then bend the wire in half. Twist the two ends of wire together and thread the beads.

Slipping beads

The easiest way to knit with beads is the slip stitch technique, which can be used for almost any size of ornament. It is worked on the right side of stocking stitch.

Knit to the stitch where you want the bead, and bring the yarn to the front. Slide the bead along the yarn and push it firmly up against the needle. Slip the stitch purlwise, take the yarn to the back and knit the next stitch. This leaves the bead suspended in front of a stitch.

Beaded knitted fabric
Beading alternate stitches on alternate rows gives this all-over effect. Slip several stitches to accommodate a large bead or bugle bead.

Knitting sequins

Sequins can also be worked by the slip stitch technique, but they lie better if they are worked into a stitch. This is done on the wrong side of stocking stitch.

Purl to the stitch where you want the sequin, insert the needle, take the yarn around the needle in the usual way, then slide a sequin down to the needle. Complete the purl stitch, pushing the sequin through to the right side of the work. Secure the sequin on the next row by knitting into the back of the stitch.

Sequinned knitted fabric
Sequins are flexible and can be pushed through a stitch more easily than beads. Closely worked beads or sequins can be used for bands and edgings as well as the whole fabric.

Slip Stitch Colour Knitting

If you want to create multicoloured knits but are worried about handling more than one colour yarn at a time, then slip stitch colour patterns are the answer because only one colour is used in a row.

These patterns are an easy way to create colour effects, because the slip stitches are slipped to take the colour over two rows — you do not need to strand colours along the row. For a reversible pattern, you may need to work two consecutive rows in the same direction, so use a circular needle or double-pointed needles in order to slide the stitches along to work from the other end.

Gingham mouse
The trousers of this charming knitted mouse are worked in gingham check.

Gingham check

MULTIPLE OF 4 STITCHES PLUS 2

Stitches are purled on all wrong-side rows, so this pretty check looks like stranded colour knitting. When choosing colours for a true gingham effect, yarn A should be the medium tone.

Colours A, B and C.
Cast on with A.
Row 1 (RS): Using A, k.
Row 2: Using B, p2, [sl 2 wyif, p2] to end.
Row 3: Using B, k2, [sl 2 wyib, k2] to end.
Row 4: Using A, p.
Row 5: Using C, sl 2 wyib, [k2, sl 2 wyib] to end.
Row 6: Using C, sl 2 wyif, [p2, sl 2 wyif] to end.
These six rows form the pattern.

Spotted stripes

MULTIPLE OF 4 STITCHES PLUS 1

By slipping stitches and sliding at row ends, you can achieve the effect of spots in the stripes. On the other side, the colours are reversed. After the first few rows, it is very easy to keep your place in this pattern.

Circular needle. Colours A and B.
Cast on with A, slide.
Row 1: Using B, p1, [k1, p1, sl 1 wyib, p1] to end, turn.
Row 2: Using B, k1, [sl 1 wyif, k1, p1, k1] to end, slide.
Row 3: Using A, k1, [p1, k1] to end, turn.
Row 4: Using A, p1, [k1, p1] to end, slide.
Row 5: Using B, p1, [k1, sl 1 wyif, k1, p1] to end, turn.
Row 6: Using B, k1, [p1, sl 1 wyib, p1, k1] to end, slide.
Row 7: Using A, as 3rd row, turn.
Row 8: Using A, as 4th row, slide.
These eight rows form the pattern.

Loops

Making an even, looped pile over the surface as you knit is a fascinating process. Much of the final effect depends on the type of yarn used and whether the loops are cut or uncut. Loops are usually worked on alternate rows so that they all lie on the right side of the fabric. The density depends on whether the loops are made with one or more strands of yarn and whether they are worked on every stitch or on alternate stitches. Experiment with these two techniques to decide which suits your yarn.

Single loops
These loops have been worked in cream wool and cut to give a sheepskin effect.

Double loops
These loops have been worked in a textured stretch yarn for a close-pile surface.

Single loops
This is a very secure loop that can be cut without unravelling. It is made on right-side rows of stocking stitch or garter stitch.

1 Knit a stitch, but do not slip it off the needle. Bring the yarn to the front between the needles; take it clockwise around your left thumb and back between the needles. Knit the stitch on the left needle again and slip it off in the usual way.

2 Insert the left needle into the front of the two new stitches on the right needle and knit them together through the back of the loops. When the knitting is finished, the loops can be cut or left uncut.

Double loops
Clusters of loops can be made on wrong-side rows of garter stitch. These clusters consist of two loops, but you can make triple loops in the same way. Do not cut the loops.

Holding yarn in the right hand
Insert the needle into the next stitch and wrap the yarn as if to knit, then wrap the yarn twice around the first two fingers of the left hand and the needle. Draw the three loops through the stitch. Insert the left needle into the loops and knit into the back and front of them, then lift the first loop over the second and off the needle. This locks the loops fairly securely.

Holding yarn in the left hand
Insert the needle into the next stitch as if to knit, catch the yarn with the right needle, then wrap the yarn twice around the first two fingers of the right hand and the needle, ending with the yarn behind the fingers. Draw the three loops through the stitch and secure the loops as described above.

Tucks and Pleats

Knitted fabrics need not be flat. You can make three-dimensional effects like tucks and pleats without using a sewing needle.

Tucks

Tucks are usually worked in stocking stitch and are similar in construction to a hem. On the right side, fold the knitting along a row and knit each stitch on the needle together with the back loop of each corresponding stitch of a previous row. Stitches can be joined across the row to give a corded effect or to make a casing. You can use small groups of stitches to make bobbles. For a small bobble, turn, work five rows on three stitches, then join by knitting these stitches together with the three of the first row.

True pleats

Plan your pleats in stocking stitch and define the folds with slip stitches on right-side rows. Slip one stitch with the yarn in front for an inside fold; slip one stitch with the yarn at the back for an outside fold. At the top of the pleat, divide the stitches into three – for the face, turn-back and underside. Slip these groups on to double-pointed needles and turn the needles to fold the fabric. Knit one stitch from each of the three needles together each time to close the top. Tack the pleats before pressing.

Mock pleats

The curl of knit stitches rolling over purl stitches can be used to make a pleated fabric. These stitch patterns are based on rib, so they also make the fabric narrower and longer.

SEE ALSO
• **Facings and hems, pages 44–45**
• **Tree and flags stitch pattern, page 60**

Mock pleats
To knit this kilted pleat effect, refer to the tree and flags pattern in the knit and purl stitch collection. Cast on a multiple of eight stitches and repeat the stitches of one flag pattern only.

Tucks
From the top, the bobbles are actually small tucks and the cord below them is only four rows deep. The next tuck has a picot edge and the heavier tuck below it has a purl ridge along the fold.

True pleats
This technique can be used to make knife-edge pleats, box pleats or inverted pleats.

Entrelac

The entrelac technique looks like magic, with the changing direction of the stitches making a woven fabric.

Entrelac uses the techniques of turning rows, increasing and decreasing, and picking up stitches to create a patchwork that is actually knitted all in one. Each block has twice as many rows as stitches – the number of stitches used to make the base triangles determines the size of the blocks. You can use any stitch pattern you want, as long as the repeat or motif fits the number of stitches and rows for each block.

SEE ALSO
• **Decreases and increases, pages 28–34**
• **Picking up stitches, page 31**
• **Turning rows, page 37**

Basic technique
The best way to understand the entrelac technique is to knit up a sample. This swatch of stocking stitch entrelacs is based on a multiple of 12 stitches. Use any yarn with appropriate size needles, but change colour for each row of blocks to emphasise the change in direction of knitting.

Starting row of base triangles
Using first colour, cast on 36 sts.
First base triangle: P2, turn, k2, turn, p3, turn, k3, turn. Purling one more stitch from left needle each time, continue in this way until there are 12 sts on right needle.
Do not turn. Leave these stitches and work two more base triangles.

First row of blocks
Change to second colour. The first row of blocks has side triangles.
First side triangle: K2, turn, p2, turn, kf&b, skpo, turn, p3, turn, kf&b, k1, skpo, turn, p4, turn. Decreasing one stitch from base triangle on knit rows each time, continue until kf&b, k9, skpo has been worked, do not turn, leave these 12 sts.
Block: Pick up and knit 12 sts from row ends of base triangle, turn, p12, turn, k11, skpo, turn, p12. Continue in this way until all sts of base triangle have been decreased; do not turn. Work a second block between second and third base triangles.
Second side triangle: Pick up and knit 12 sts from row ends of last base triangle, turn, p2 tog, p10, turn, k11, turn, p2 tog, p9, turn, k10. Continue decreasing at beginning of every purl row until 1 st remains, turn, slip st on to left needle.

Second row of blocks
Change to first colour. The second row of blocks does not have side triangles.
Block: P1, pick up and purl 11 sts, turn, k12, turn, p11, p2 tog, turn, k12. Continue in this way until all stitches of first row block have been decreased; do not turn.
Work remaining blocks in this way.

Motif entrelac
The little boats look as if they are going up and down on the waves because of the different directions of the knitting. The opening and closing triangles are in contrast colours. Each block of this entrelac is worked on 12 stitches and each boat motif is 9 stitches wide, leaving the edges clear for joining the blocks.

Continuing to work entrelac
The next row of blocks is the same as the first row of blocks, but working into the second row of blocks instead of base triangles. Alternating colours, work as many rows of blocks as you want, but always end with a first row of blocks, then finish off with triangles to give a straight edge at the top.

Last row of blocks
Change to first colour.
Closing triangles: P1, pick up and purl 11 sts from row ends of side triangle, turn, k12, turn, p2 tog, p9, p2 tog, turn, k11, turn, p2 tog, p8, p2 tog, turn, k10, turn. Continue in this way until turn, k2 has been worked, turn, p1, p2 tog, turn, k2, turn, p3 tog, 1 st remains.
Picking up and purling 11 sts from row ends of blocks, work second and third closing triangles.

Entrelac with cables
Adding a cable to your entrelac is fun. This swatch is based on a multiple of 12 stitches, but to balance the pattern, you will need an extra edge stitch. Increase 1 st on the first row and decrease it on the last row of each block to work this 6-stitch cable with 2 sts in reverse stocking stitch on each side.

Facings and Hems

Instead of working edges in rib or garter stitch, you can make hems or facings for a more substantial double-fabric finish.

The addition of facings or hems really needs to be considered before you start to knit. It is possible to knit from an edge to produce a facing or hem, but there will be a join that may be difficult to disguise. These techniques owe more to dressmaking than to knitting, but they can be very successful if the right design and yarn are chosen.

SEE ALSO
- **Basic cast-ons, pages 16–17**
- **Casting off, pages 22–23**
- **Decreases and increases, pages 28–34**

Plain hem

A knitted hem can be turned up and sewn in place in the same way as a woven fabric hem. However, this can be bulky and the folded edge may spread, so it is preferable to make a neat knitted-in hem.

With smaller needles than for the main piece, cast on fairly loosely using the loop method. Work the depth of the hem in stocking stitch. Mark the fold with a ridge by working a row out of sequence – either three purl rows or three knit rows, the centre row of the three making the ridge. Change to the needles for the main piece and continue in stocking stitch until the depth from the ridge matches that of the hem, ending with a purl row. To join the hem on the next row, fold the hem up behind the main piece, then knit together the first stitch from the left needle with the first stitch from the cast-on edge. Continue in this way to the end of the row.

Picot hem
The stitches between the eyelets form the picots when the hem is turned up.

Picot hem

A very attractive way to mark the fold of a hem is to work a row of eyelets that, when the hem is turned up, make a row of well-defined picots. Work to the depth of the hem, ending with a wrong-side row.

If there is an odd number of stitches, work the next row as k1, *yo, k2 tog, rep from * to end. Over an even number of stitches, work the row as k2, *yo, k2 tog, rep from * to end.

Facings

Unlike ribbon or woven fabric, a knitted stocking stitch facing will be flexible and a perfect colour match. For the front edges of a jacket or cardigan, it is best to work the facing as part of the main piece. To ensure that the facing folds on the same stitch along its length, slip this stitch on every right-side row.

Facing
A line of slip stitches forms a natural fold line for a facing.

Fastenings

Mitred corners

Where a hem and facing meet, or between an edging and a front band, a mitred corner may be the neatest solution. For this you need to increase or decrease to make a 45-degree angle. Shaping on alternate rows in garter stitch or moss stitch produces this angle almost perfectly. In stocking stitch, achieving the correct angle may entail shaping on a mixture of alternate rows and every row, because the stitches are wider than they are tall.

Mitred corner
The garter stitch edging and front band form a neatly mitred corner.

Fastenings are details you should consider before you start knitting and perhaps work a swatch for. If you are knitting a project that requires some form of fastening, here is how to make it as neat as possible.

Securing a button with a shank
Faced front edges or a chunky yarn may require the button to have a shank. To make the shank, sew on the button over a spacer such as a cable needle. When the button is secure, remove the spacer, twist the yarn around the shank, then fasten off.

Buttonholes with a facing
One buttonhole in the main piece and one buttonhole in the facing come together when the facing is turned in along the line of slip stitches.

Buttonholes

Buttonholes are best kept simple. Knitted fabric does not lend itself to the detailed finishing used on woven fabric, so try to make buttonholes neat enough so that hand sewing with buttonhole stitch afterwards is unnecessary, because this reduces size and flexibility and can be clumsy. Choose the buttons first and make the buttonholes to fit.

Eyelet buttonholes

A single or double eyelet is often sufficient for a small buttonhole. A single eyelet is made with a yarn over and single decrease; a double eyelet is made with a double yarn over and a balanced single decrease on either side.

Horizontal buttonholes

The simplest method is to cast off stitches on one row with a chain cast-off, and cast on the same number above them on the next row with a backward loop cast-on. To prevent a hole before the first stitch of the cast-on group, work into the front and back of the last stitch before the buttonhole, and cast on one stitch less.

Vertical buttonholes

Knit along the row to the place where the buttonhole will be, turn, then work the required number of rows. Break the yarn, rejoin it where the knitting turned and work the same number of rows on this side. Finally, work on all stitches to close the buttonhole at the top. Use the two ends of yarn left to reinforce the top and base of the buttonhole.

Zips

Zips are slightly incompatible with knitting, but they are sometimes more appropriate than buttons. Edge the zip opening with a few stitches of garter stitch or moss stitch. Pin and tack the zip in place, lining up rows or stitch patterns on either side. Open the zip to back stitch it. For a neat finish, knit narrow facings to cover the tape of the zip.

Making Up

Assembling a knitted garment involves two processes – pressing or blocking each piece of knitting, then sewing the pieces together.

Pressing

Pinning out and pressing your knitting before sewing up will make an enormous difference to the finished garment. Always check the ball band for yarn care, and test a sample swatch before applying heat or steam to your knitting – natural fibre yarns are usually quite robust, but man-made mixes can collapse and therefore need a cool, dry iron.

Pin each piece out to size with right side down on a padded board, using a tape measure to check the measurement. Cover the board with a checked fabric to help you line up the rows and stitches. Then lay a dampened cotton cloth on top, and gently apply the iron. Never stamp the iron down or push it along the knitting. Knitting can be moulded into shape at the pressing stage if it is wool or cotton. Buy or make a tailor's ham – an overstuffed fabric ball – for pressing set-in sleeve heads.

Blocking

If the yarn is delicate or if the stitch pattern is textured, pin out the pieces but do not press. Instead, dampen them with a water spray, then allow them to dry naturally – a process known as blocking.

Sewing up

This takes time to do properly, so do not be tempted to rush this process. Using small safety pins, long sewing pins – quilter's pins are ideal – or a length of contrasting yarn threaded on to a tapestry needle, secure any points that should align on the project. If you are using safety pins, use them horizontally to the edge rather than parallel to the edge – this leaves the fabric more flexible. This can be done with normal pins, but they tend to get in the way if they protrude beyond an edge.

You do not have to use the same stitch to sew up all the seams. Consider each seam carefully and then, in a good light, try to match the edges stitch for stitch along their length. In general, even, regular stitching will be less noticeable. After sewing a project together, lightly press or steam the reverse side of the project again using a damp cloth.

Mattress stitch seam on stocking stitch
The seam is almost invisible in stocking stitch.

Mattress stitch seam on rib
Ribbing needs to be planned so that, when the seam is joined, the stitches at each edge combine to make a whole rib.

Mattress stitch seam on striped fabric
Stripes and colour patterns are easier to match when sewn together from the right side.

Neat drop shoulders
If you are joining a straight cast-off sleeve top to the row ends of a back and front to make a drop shoulder, do not match stitch for stitch. Skip a few row ends at regular intervals to compensate for the different stitch and row tensions.

Mattress stitch

This method, also known as invisible seam or ladder stitch, is good for joining side and sleeve seams in most stitch patterns.

Place both pieces of knitting flat, with right sides facing and the edges to be joined vertical. Thread a blunt-ended sewing needle with yarn and secure at one lower edge – the first side. Take the needle under the cast-on edge of the second side, draw the yarn through, then go under the first cast-on edge again. Tension the yarn to level the edges. Take the needle under the strand between the edge stitch and the next stitch on the first row of the second side, and draw the yarn through. Repeat for the first row of the first side. Continue joining row ends from alternate sides in this way, without splitting stitches.

Edge-to-edge mattress stitch

This technique is useful for joining shoulders. The stitches run in opposite directions, so the side edges will be a half-stitch out, but this can be hidden in a seam.

Thread a blunt-ended sewing needle with yarn and bring it up through the centre of the first stitch on the front. Take it under the edge stitch on the back and down through the first stitch again. Repeat, taking in a whole stitch each time to match the front and back stitches perfectly.

Slip stitch

Slip stitch is a particularly light way to seam. It is useful for catching down pocket linings as well as to secure facings.

With wrong sides facing, tack the pieces to be joined, matching rows. Thread a blunt-ended sewing needle with yarn. Secure the end, then take the needle alternately under a strand on the main fabric and an edge strand. Do not let the stitches show on the right side or pull the yarn too tight.

Back stitch

Back stitch creates a strong seam that is ideal for seams that may need to bear some weight. It is also a useful embroidery stitch.

Hold the pieces with right sides together. Thread a blunt-ended sewing needle with yarn and secure it at the right-hand end. Lining up rows and working one stitch in from the edge, bring the needle up through both pieces between stitches of the first and second rows, then down between the first row and cast-on edge. Come up again one or two rows on, and go down next to the previous stitch. Complete the seam in this way, working between the knitted stitches.

WEAVING IN YARN ENDS

All pieces of knitting begin and end with a tail of yarn, and more are created when you join in a new ball, change colours and sew up seams. These yarn ends need to be woven into the wrong side of the knitted fabric using a blunt-ended sewing needle. Most can be woven along a seam, but some may have to be woven in and out of the back of a few stitches. Make sure that they do not show through on the right side of the fabric. Trim any excess yarn.

Pocket linings

To keep pocket linings square when stitching them down, tack contrast colour guidelines between the stitches on each side of the pocket opening on the right side of the fabric. Turn over and follow the tacked guidelines to sew the pocket linings down.

Kitchener Stitch

Also referred to as grafting or weaving, this technique is used to join two sets of uncast-off stitches together without creating a visible seam. The technique can also be used to alter the length of a garment.

Commonly used to join shoulders, Kitchener stitch involves duplicating a row of stitches using yarn and a blunt-ended sewing needle. Always use a blunt needle to avoid splitting stitches. Thread the needle with a length of matching yarn three times the width of the row.

Getting started

Lay the pieces to be joined close together, with the knitting needles pointing in the same direction and the uncast-off stitches near the tips so that you can slip them off the needles easily as you trap them with the sewn stitches. The Kitchener stitches should be tensioned to match the knitting, but you can go back once the row has been completed and ease the stitches.

ADJUSTING THE LENGTH OF THE KNITTED FABRIC
Examine the fabric and look for a discreet place to add or subtract rows. The start or end of a pattern change usually works well. To make the alteration, snip a stitch in the centre of the row, then pick up the loops of the stitches above and the stitches of the row below as you ease out the yarn. Use two needles, one to pick up the stitches below and the other for the loops above. Using the two ends of a circular needle may make picking up stitches easier.

Working on the stitches of the lower piece, undo rows to make it shorter or add more rows to make it longer. Then use Kitchener stitch to join the two sections together again.

Working Kitchener stitch

It is easiest to Kitchener stitch in stocking stitch or reverse stocking stitch, but once you understand how to imitate knit and purl stitches, you can using Kitchener stitch to graft pieces in other stitch patterns.

Knit Kitchener stitch
Lay the pieces to be joined flat, knit side facing you. The sewn stitches will make a knit row.

Bring the needle up through the first stitch of the last row on the lower piece. Go down through the loop at the side edge and up in the centre of the next loop on the upper piece, then go down through the first stitch of the lower piece again and up through the next stitch. Continue until all stitches and loops are joined to make a row.

Purl Kitchener stitch
Lay the pieces to be joined flat, purl side facing you. The sewn stitches will make a purl row.

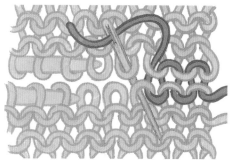

Bring the needle down through the first stitch on the lower piece, up through the loop at the side edge and down in the centre of the next loop on the upper piece. Then go up through the first stitch of the lower piece. Continue in this way along the row, tensioning the sewn stitches as you go.

Garter Kitchener stitch
To keep the pattern correct, make sure that the lower piece of knitting ends with a ridge and the upper piece with a smooth row. To join the pieces, work the lower stitches as for knit Kitchener stitch and the upper stitches as for purl Kitchener stitch.

Rib Kitchener stitch
Follow the pattern of the stitches, alternating knit and purl Kitchener stitch. Wide ribs are easier to join than single rib.

Embroidery

Embroidery has a great affinity with hand knitting. You can use the same yarn, a contrast yarn or an embroidery thread. Embroidery doubles the thickness of the fabric, so it is better not to use it for large, solid areas.

Duplicate stitch

Also known as Swiss darning, this is a clever means of imitating multicolour knitting in stocking stitch.

1 Bring the needle out at the base of a stitch. Insert it from right to left under the two strands of the stitch above.

2 Take the needle into the base of the first stitch and out at the base of the next stitch. Continue making each duplicate stitch from right to left, covering knitted stitches.

TIP
Use a tapestry needle for embroidery and work between the strands of the knitting, rather than splitting the yarn.

Chain stitch

Linear designs are very effective in chain stitch. Instead of working chain stitch with a tapestry needle, try using a medium-to-fine crochet hook – it is easier and faster. Chain stitch can also look very effective worked in the same yarn and colour as the stocking stitch base.

1 Hold the thread underneath the work with your free hand and hold the crochet hook above. Take the hook down through the knitting and pull up a loop of yarn.

2 Insert the hook in the next stitch and pull up a second loop through the first. Continue in this way, working between knitted strands.

Chain stitch motifs

These motifs were made freely with no guidelines. If you want to work a vertical line, perhaps up a rib, skip a strand occasionally to keep the chain lying flat.

Eyelets

Single and double eyelets in stocking stitch can be overcast with matching or contrasting stranded tapestry yarn. Work the eyelets at random or embellish a lace stitch pattern. Use a single strand of tapestry yarn to make a line of running stitches around the eyelet, then overcast the running stitches and the edge of the eyelet.

Cross stitch

Cross stitch embroidery works beautifully on stocking stitch. Each cross stitch covers a single knitted stitch. However, knitted stitches are wider than they are tall, so the cross stitches will not be square. Take this into account when choosing or drawing a chart.

Stitch Collection

This chapter features design ideas and inspiration themed by stitch style. The introductory pages for each style discuss key aspects of the techniques involved, followed by a number of carefully selected stitch patterns to inform and inspire you further.

From basic knit and purl combinations to intricate lacework, and from highly textured cable and twist stitches to smooth stranded and intarsia colourwork, this chapter includes more than 150 stitch patterns to help you develop your technical skills and inspire your knitting designs.

On pages 156–157 you will find guidance on how to follow the charts for the stitch patterns, plus a key to all the symbols used. Any additional symbols are explained next to the pattern.

◄ ELISA VANDERSCHUIT
KNITTED CABLE BLANKET
Cable patterns are ideal for cosy blankets and throws. Knitted on giant needles using doubled-up super-chunky yarn, this blanket features a large cable panel running down the centre with narrower panels of garter stitch along each side. Tassels at each end of the blanket provide additional texture.

Knit and purl

Knit and purl stitch patterns can be used to create anything from cushions and traditional sweaters to fashion designs in crunchy textures and subtle brocades — the possibilities are endless.

Alternate knit and purl and you get the simplest texture stitches. Group the knits and purls geometrically to make blocks, diagonals, chevrons and diamonds, or put them together more freely to create motifs. Patterns can be repeated to make an all-over design, or used in panels with simple stitch patterns between.

On a practical level, a mixture of knit and purl stitches on a row or up a column of stitches creates a flatter fabric — one less prone to the curling of stocking stitch or the contracting of many rib stitch patterns. This characteristic is often used in edging stitch patterns and for collars and facings.

On the right side of the fabric, the knit stitches appear smooth, while each purl stitch makes a little blip. If you think of the smooth stitches as light and the blips as dark, you will find it easy to read the charts on the following pages.

SEE ALSO
• Knit and purl stitch patterns,
  pages 54–61

▼▶ JEANETTE TROTMAN
FLORAL SUMMER THROW
Made from five scarf-sized sections joined together, the solid-coloured panels feature a pattern of purl-textured rectangles, while ridges of purl stitch accentuate the stripy panels. Beads and sew-on knitted flowers add further embellishment to create a jazzy riot of colour.

Working into the back of a stitch

Working into the back of stitches is often used to add definition to a stitch pattern. It closes up the V shape on the right side of the fabric and makes the diagonals from bottom right to top left more prominent. As the knitting progresses, these diagonals emphasise the verticals on the right side of the fabric.

To knit into the back of a stitch
Insert the right needle into the back of the stitch from right to left, take the yarn around the needle and make the new stitch in the usual way.

To purl into the back of a stitch
Swing the needle ends slightly away from you to insert the right needle into the back of the stitch from left to right, then take the yarn around the needle and make a new stitch in the usual way.

Crossed stocking stitch
To work crossed stocking stitch, knit into the back of each stitch on right-side rows and purl into the back of each stitch on wrong-side rows.

Slipping a stitch

To slip a stitch, simply move it from the left to the right needle without working it. When this is done as part of a stitch pattern, the stitch is usually slipped purlwise, so that the stitch lies on the needle in the same direction as an ordinary knit stitch.

Slipping stitches makes a close, firm fabric. If the stitch is slipped purlwise on a right-side row with the yarn at the back, the design element is vertical. If the stitch is slipped purlwise on a right-side row with the yarn at the front, the design element is horizontal.

Stitches can also be slipped purlwise on wrong-side rows. If the yarn is held in front, the strand will not show on the right side; if the yarn is held at the back, the strand will show on the right side.

To slip one stitch with the yarn at the back on a knit row
Insert the right needle into the stitch as if to purl, then slip the stitch from the left to the right needle. Do not take the yarn around the needle – there is no new stitch.

To slip one stitch with the yarn at the front on a knit row
Bring the yarn to the front, insert the right needle into the stitch as if to purl, then slip the stitch from the left to the right needle. Take the yarn to the back of the work to knit the next stitch.

Barred stocking stitch
Purl on wrong-side rows; on right-side rows, knit and, holding the yarn in front, slip alternate stitches.

Moss stitch

MULTIPLE OF 2 STITCHES PLUS 1

MULTIPLE OF 2 STITCHES PLUS 2

Over an odd number of stitches, you can start moss stitch with either a knit or a purl stitch. Over an even number of stitches, if the first stitch of the first row is knit, the first stitch of the second row will be purl.

MOSS STITCH AND SEED STITCH
UK terminology is used in this book:
UK moss stitch = US seed stitch
UK double moss stitch = US moss stitch

Little blocks

MULTIPLE OF 6 STITCHES PLUS 3

Also known as basketweave stitch, patterns of alternating blocks of stocking stitch and reverse stocking stitch can be worked over any combination of stitches and rows. Block patterns have a similar tension to that of stocking stitch, so the little blocks here appear square even though there are more rows than stitches to each block.

Welting

MULTIPLE OF ANY NUMBER OF STITCHES

Welting patterns can be worked on any number of stitches, odd or even, and with any combination of rows of reverse stocking stitch and stocking stitch. This fabric spreads widthways and contracts vertically.

Broken blocks

MULTIPLE OF 8 STITCHES PLUS 10

Adding a garter ridge to the stocking stitch blocks makes this pattern look more exciting than plain blocks, yet it is very easy to work.

Double moss stitch

MULTIPLE OF 2 STITCHES PLUS 1

Double moss stitch is extremely useful because the row tension is similar to that of stocking stitch, which makes it ideal for creating textured motifs on a stocking stitch background (see double moss stitch star and heart on page 58). The chart shows double moss stitch beginning with purl, because this holds the corner of the knitting more neatly. If double moss stitch is to be used after p1, k1 rib, then start with a knit stitch, as in the third row of the chart.

Tiny double moss diamonds

MULTIPLE OF 6 STITCHES PLUS 1

This stitch shows the smallest possible double moss stitch diamonds on stocking stitch. Use it as an all-over pattern, or work just three or four repeats for a textured panel.

Cornish lattice

MULTIPLE OF 6 STITCHES PLUS 3

This stitch pattern is based on purl garter stitch and stocking stitch, which makes it easy to work.

Garter diamonds

MULTIPLE OF 20 STITCHES PLUS 1

Although the large repeat makes this pattern look complicated, it is easy to work because it is made with knit and purl stitches on right-side rows, and every wrong-side row is just purl.

Twisted little check

MULTIPLE OF 10 STITCHES PLUS 1

Working the stocking stitch squares through the back of the loops gives a lovely definition to the blocks.

Twisted diagonal

MULTIPLE OF 8 STITCHES PLUS 2

You could work the stocking stitch part of this pattern without twisting the stitches, but the result would be less well-defined diagonals. For a diagonal running to the right, reverse the chart.

Twisted chevron

MULTIPLE OF 12 STITCHES PLUS 1

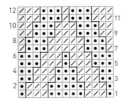

When diagonals are worked in alternate directions, they meet to make chevrons. Working stitches through the back of the loops makes the chevrons appear taller and more elegant.

Twisted square check

MULTIPLE OF 10 STITCHES PLUS 2

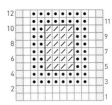

See how the small blocks of stitches, which are worked through the back of the loops, contrast with the stocking stitch outlining the blocks.

Double moss stitch star

MOTIF OF 23 STITCHES

This star can be used as a single motif, scattered on a stocking stitch background or repeated in blocks. If you are planning to use it as a repeat pattern, chart it out in full to make sure that you have allowed enough extra stocking stitch background stitches between the stars.

Double moss stitch heart

MOTIF OF 25 STITCHES

This heart motif can be used in the same way as the moss stitch star (left) or combined with other stitch patterns. It is very easy to make this motif larger – simply copy the design on to graph paper, then add more pairs of dots for purl stitches evenly all around the motif until the heart is the size you want.

Linen stitch

MULTIPLE OF 2 STITCHES PLUS 3

This densely woven fabric is made by slipping stitches on both right- and wrong-side rows. Remember to bring the yarn forwards before slipping a stitch on right-side rows, and to take the yarn back before slipping a stitch on wrong-side rows, so that the strands always appear on the right side of the work.

Slip stitch herringbone

MULTIPLE OF 8 STITCHES PLUS 7

Slipping two stitches creates the horizontal strands in this subtle pattern. When you are slipping two stitches, it is easier to slip them purlwise together. Do not strand too tightly, because it will pull in and make a very thick fabric.

Butterfly blocks

MULTIPLE OF 10 STITCHES PLUS 7

Ⓤ Take right needle under the three long strands and knit them with the stitch.

Stranded fabrics are not all heavy. In this pattern, also called bowknot, the long strands are linked into a knit stitch to make a lively variation on simple blocks.

Tree and flags

MULTIPLE OF 40 STITCHES PLUS 1

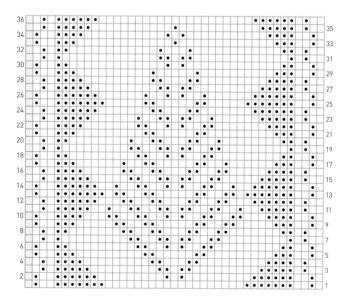

Note the way the flag panels just miss touching the tree. The busy little pattern between the flag panels is simply double moss stitch.

Hearts and chevrons

PANEL OF 5 STITCHES / 11 STITCHES / 5 STITCHES / 15 STITCHES

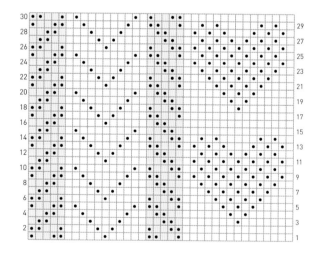

These diagonal, chevron and heart patterns can all be used as separate panels. The chevron panel is a 10-row repeat, so it fits neatly into the 30-row repeat of the heart panel. The tiny diagonals repeat every 4 rows, so you will need to work 60 rows before the pattern repeats exactly.

Diamond and net

MULTIPLE OF 42 STITCHES PLUS 3

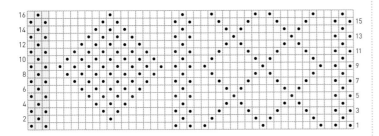

The moss stitch diamond is so satisfying because its shape echoes the diamond contained in the crisscross of the net.

Daisy

MOTIF OF 25 STITCHES

Knit and purl stitches can be used to draw naturalistic motifs, using the play of light on the surface of the knitting to define the design. If you want a daisy leaning in the opposite direction, copy the chart on to graph paper in reverse. For a smooth-petalled daisy on a textured background, all you have to do is reverse the knit and purl stitches.

Rib

Simple ribs are combinations of knit and purl stitches that form verticals and contract the knitting across the width.

In rib, the knit stitches are raised and the purl stitches sink down. The resulting elasticity makes rib very suitable for edgings and cuffs. Some ribbed garments are designed to fit closely, but choice of yarn is important. Wool, for example, will make a springy, stretchy rib, while cotton ribs will lie flat. In the wrong yarn, a skinny rib sweater just will not cling.

Ribs are usually worked on needles one, two or more sizes smaller than for other stitches. The smaller the needle size, the more the rib will contract. Interesting patterns can be made by combining simple rib with cable, lace and twist stitches.

Measuring the length of a piece of ribbing can be difficult, because this measurement will vary depending on whether the knitting is stretched or contracted widthways. In the end, it is best to measure ribs half-stretched unless the instructions state otherwise.

SEE ALSO
• **Rib stitch patterns, pages 64–71**

• Rib stitch patterns, pages 64–71

BAGGY RIB STITCHES
In rib patterns, the knit stitch that immediately precedes a purl stitch is often a bit larger than the others. One solution is to work this knit stitch slightly more firmly. Another option is to knit into the back of this knit stitch, then wrap the yarn clockwise around the needle rather than anticlockwise when working the following purl stitch.

Rib yoke
The yoke of this child's cardigan is worked in a series of offset rib patterns. The elastic rib ensures a perfect fit and the purl troughs are an excellent place to discreetly work the increases.

Popular rib patterns and variations

There are some rib patterns, such as single rib, double rib and broken double rib, whose versatility and durability make them a popular choice.

There are several more stitch patterns – such as fisherman's rib and brioche rib – that, at first glance, have the appearance of one of the more popular ribs but are in fact more than just a combination of knit and purl stitches.

Single rib
For this basic rib, alternate knit and purl stitches are worked above each other.

Over an even number of stitches:
Repeat k1, p1 to the end of each row.

Over an odd number of stitches:
Begin k1, then repeat p1, k1 to the end. On alternate rows begin p1, then k1, p1 to the end.

Double rib
Knit two, purl two rib makes a very elastic fabric with strongly defined ridges and furrows. This rib can be worked on a number of stitches divisible by four, in which case k2, p2 is repeated along each row. To balance it at each end, work on a number of stitches divisible by four, plus two. The first row begins k2 and is followed by p2, k2 repeated to the end. The second row begins p2, followed by k2, p2 to the end.

Broken double rib
This variation on double rib does not pull in. The right side of the fabric is worked as a double rib and on the purl side all the stitches are purled.

Fisherman's rib
Fisherman's rib is an interesting variation on single rib. Knitting alternate stitches in the row below gives a deeper, softer rib. It is often confused with brioche rib, which is slightly loftier.

The stitch is knitted in the usual way, except that the point of the right needle goes into the stitch directly underneath the first stitch on the left needle. Both strands are then dropped off the needle together.

Brioche rib
Brioche rib is made with slip stitches and yarn overs; there are no purl stitches. Instructions are charted on page 71.

When knitting together a slip stitch and a yarn over, the two strands are already in place on the needle and are knitted together in the usual way.

Single rib

MULTIPLE OF 2 STITCHES PLUS 1

Alternate knit and purl stitches make up this rib. It is also called knit one, purl one rib or one-and-one rib.

Broken single rib

MULTIPLE OF 2 STITCHES PLUS 1

Purling the wrong-side rows reduces the elasticity of the rib and produces an attractive texture.

Twisted single rib

MULTIPLE OF 2 STITCHES PLUS 1

This well-defined rib has the knit stitches on the right side and the purl stitches on the wrong side worked through the back of the loops.

Double rib

MULTIPLE OF 4 STITCHES PLUS 2

Also known as knit two, purl two rib or two-and-two rib, this classic stitch is the same on both sides.

Broken double rib

MULTIPLE OF 4 STITCHES PLUS 2

Purling wrong-side rows turns classic double rib into a firm fabric with verticals of stocking stitch and garter stitch.

Bamboo rib

MULTIPLE OF 8 STITCHES PLUS 6

Interspersing the double rib pattern with small bands of welting makes an interesting variation on a familiar theme.

Diagonal double rib

MULTIPLE OF 4 STITCHES

Moving the double rib pattern along one stitch on alternate rows produces well-defined diagonals.

Wide rib

MULTIPLE OF 8 STITCHES PLUS 2

A wide rib can comprise any number of stitches. This one combines six of stocking stitch with two of reverse stocking stitch.

Welted rib

MULTIPLE OF 6 STITCHES

Joining up single ribs with small blocks of welting makes an all-over diagonal pattern.

Shadow rib

MULTIPLE OF 3 STITCHES PLUS 2

Knitting a stitch through the back of the loop on right-side rows creates a neat little blip on a reverse stocking stitch ground.

Close stitch

MULTIPLE OF 2 STITCHES PLUS 1

Slipped stitches make this gentle rib very thick and soft – ideal for socks.

Crossed rib

MULTIPLE OF 3 STITCHES PLUS 1

Sl 1 knitwise, k in front and back of next st, pass sl st over.

Although it looks like a twisted rib, this effect is achieved by passing a slipped stitch over an increase.

Stocking heel rib

MULTIPLE OF 2 STITCHES PLUS 1

This stitch pattern is used to reinforce sock and stocking heels.

Moss and slip stitch rib

MULTIPLE OF 6 STITCHES PLUS 5

Moss stitch panels make this slip stitch rib extra firm and substantial.

Cartridge belt rib

MULTIPLE OF 4 STITCHES PLUS 3

Slipping stitches on both sides of the knitting gives well-defined ridges and a fabric that is the same on both sides.

Moss rib

MULTIPLE OF 6 STITCHES PLUS 1

Another reversible stitch, this combines single rib and moss stitch.

Broken moss rib

MULTIPLE OF 10 STITCHES PLUS 3

Dividing stocking stitch panels with moss stitch gives a flat, mock rib.

Embossed rib

MULTIPLE OF 4 STITCHES PLUS 3

This firm rib combines stitches worked through the back of the loops with a nubbly knit and purl texture.

Double moss rib

MULTIPLE OF 6 STITCHES PLUS 1

Panels of double moss stitch alternate with single rib.

Double moss diamond rib

MULTIPLE OF 10 STITCHES PLUS 3

Both sides of this rib are attractive. On the reverse, the diamonds sit on a stocking stitch background and the ribs are less conspicuous.

Fisherman's rib

MULTIPLE OF 2 STITCHES PLUS 3

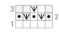

Ⅴ   K in row below.

Knitting alternate stitches in the row below is the secret of this deep, soft rib. Both sides look the same. After working row 1, repeat only rows 2 and 3.

Brioche rib

MULTIPLE OF 2 STITCHES PLUS 3

⊖ Yfwd, sl 1 purlwise, take yarn over needle.

△ K tog the sl st and yo.

This rib looks similar to fisherman's rib but is made quite differently.

Tilted rib

MULTIPLE OF 42 STITCHES PLUS 8

Panels of diagonal ribs are made with increases and decreases.

▽ Purl into front of stitch, then k into back of stitch.

Cables

Knitting groups of stitches out of sequence creates some of the world's most exciting stitch patterns. Cables can be worked with two or more stitches, and they can be crossed to the front or the back to make hundreds of coiling and interlacing patterns.

Cable stitches are most commonly associated with Aran sweaters, the traditional fisherman's sweaters from the Aran Islands off the coast of Ireland, in which panels of ropes, braids, diamonds, trellis and embossed stitches are combined to flamboyant effect.

Modern knit designers often combine cable stitches to make fascinating figurative motifs. Classic cables are more restrained and give a sophisticated touch to the plainest garment.

How to cable

Cabling involves transferring one, two or more stitches on to a short double-pointed needle. When the cable needle is held at the back, the stitches on the right side of the work make a diagonal from left to right. When the cable needle is held at the front, the stitches make a diagonal from right to left. Cable stitches can be knitted, purled or textured as directed in the pattern instructions.

Once you have mastered the techniques for basic four-stitch cables shown here, you will be able to tackle any cable stitch pattern. You will also find it easy to customise cables, such as making them wider or taller, or cabling more frequently for a firmer fabric or less often for a softer effect.

SEE ALSO
- **Texture and pattern, page 148**
- **Cable stitch patterns, pages 74–81**

◀ **ALISON DUPERNEX**
PATCHWORK CABLE BLANKET
Large squares worked in five different textured stitch patterns – including cables, twist stitches and knot stitches – are seamed together to make this patchwork sampler blanket.

> **TIP**
> Counting rows between cables can be tricky. Slip a marker of contrast yarn between stitches on the cable row and pull it out afterwards.

Back cable

This four-stitch cable crosses at the back and all the stitches are knitted.

1 Slip the first two stitches on to a cable needle and hold at the back of the work, then knit the next two stitches from the left needle.

2 Knit the two stitches from the cable needle.

Back purl cable

This four-stitch cable has knit stitches making a diagonal to the right on a purl background.

1 Slip the first two stitches on to a cable needle and hold at the back of the work, then knit the next two stitches from the left needle.

2 Purl the two stitches from the cable needle.

Front cable

All the stitches are knitted, but this four-stitch cable crosses at the front.

1 Slip the first two stitches on to a cable needle and hold at the front of the work, then knit the next two stitches from the left needle.

2 Knit the two stitches from the cable needle.

Front purl cable

This four-stitch cable has knit stitches making a diagonal to the left on a purl background.

1 Slip the first two stitches on to a cable needle and hold at the front of the work, then purl the next two stitches from the left needle.

2 Knit the two stitches from the cable needle.

Braids and ropes

MULTIPLE OF 28 STITCHES

Little cables worked over four rows are fine on their own, but are especially good for slipping in between bigger panels. Here, they are used with eight-row braids.

Four-strand braid and snake cables

PANEL OF 44 STITCHES

This panel is surprisingly easy to work, because all the wrong-side rows are just purl. There is no limit to the number of strands you can braid – just add six more stitches for each strand.

Oxo and honeycomb

PANEL OF 44 STITCHES

The centre panel of honeycomb cable has a repeat of eight stitches, so you could work it over any multiple of eight to make it wider or narrower.

Cable check

MULTIPLE OF 12 STITCHES PLUS 6

The three-over-three cables at the top of each block make this simple pattern of knit and purl blocks look more complicated than it really is.

Little cable ribs

MULTIPLE OF 13 STITCHES PLUS 6

Twists are often used to make two-stitch crosses, but the smooth effect created by true cabling is worth the extra work, as this pattern shows. You could make the spiral rib wider by adding any multiple of two stitches.

Triple zigzag and rope

PANEL OF 36 STITCHES

This zigzag is the worked here in groups of three, but can be worked in any number to create different effects. Reverse the rope cable if you are working a pair of panels.

Cable knot rib

MULTIPLE OF 14 STITCHES PLUS 8

This six-stitch cable alternates with a two-stitch rib. The pattern looks very busy, but it is easy to do.

Braid and rib

MULTIPLE OF 12 STITCHES PLUS 3

If you would like a fatter braid, try working over twelve stitches, cabling four over four each time.

Deckle edge

MULTIPLE OF 12 STITCHES PLUS 2

Two-over-two cables along the edges of stocking stitch panels contrast effectively with narrow bands of garter stitch. All wrong-side rows are purled.

Two-texture zigzag

MULTIPLE OF 14 STITCHES PLUS 2

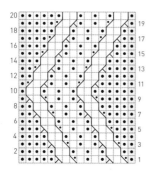

This pattern is a good one for getting used to knit and purl cables, because the purl stitch always fits into the double moss stitch. To reverse the zigzag, start the chart on row 11.

Smocked cable

PANEL OF 24 STITCHES

K4, sl all 4 sts on to cable needle and hold at front. Wind yarn tightly anticlockwise around sts on cable needle 4 times, ending at wrong side. Sl 4 sts back on to right needle.

Although smocking can be created by sewing ribs together, using cables and clusters gives better definition. This technique can be used to simulate other popular smocking designs.

Textured cable

MULTIPLE OF 16 STITCHES PLUS 10

⊠⊡⊠ Sl 3 sts on to cable needle and hold
at front, k3, then k1, p1, k1 from
cable needle.

⊠⊡⊠ Sl 3 sts on to cable needle and hold
at front, k1, p1, k1, then k3 from
cable needle.

Single rib could be substituted, with
the knit stitches worked through the
back of the loops.

Leaf cable

MULTIPLE OF 18 STITCHES PLUS 9

These cabled leaves are used here for
an all-over pattern, but they could also
be combined with other cable stitches.

Ribbed cable

PANEL OF 12 STITCHES

 Sl 3 sts on to cable needle and hold at back. K1 tbl, p1, k1 tbl, then k1 tbl, p1, k1 tbl from cable needle.

 As above, but hold cable needle at front.

Crossed stitches are worked with this ribbed cable.

Tulip cable

PANEL OF 10 STITCHES

All k sts of cables are worked tbl.

One-over-one cables and stitches crossed by working through the back of the loops form stylised flowers.

Ovals and flowers

PANEL OF 34 STITCHES

 K2, sl these 2 sts on to cable needle and hold at front. Wind yarn anticlockwise around sts on cable needle 3 times, ending at wrong side. Sl 2 sts back on to right needle.

Cabling on wrong-side rows is no harder than cabling on the right side, and because the stitches from the four-stitch cable are cabled again on the next row, they spring out cleanly.

Horseshoe trellis

MULTIPLE OF 16 STITCHES PLUS 2

Extra cables springing out of the background add interest to an all-over trellis pattern.

Brocade

PANEL OF 21 STITCHES

Sl 2 sts on to cable needle and hold at back, k2, then p1, k1 tbl from cable needle.

Sl 2 sts on to cable needle and hold at front, k1 tbl, p1, then k2 from cable needle.

Elegant curves can be made with very simple cables. This stitch pattern can be used as a panel, or staggered as a repeat.

Twists

Twists involve working two or three stitches out of sequence, but without using a cable needle. This is an easy way to create patterns where lines of stitches travel over the surface of the knitting.

Some twist stitch patterns look like miniature cables, while others create diagonals, zigzags and diamonds. Twisting stitches closes up the work, so densely twisted stitch patterns can make the fabric thicker and less flexible – unless larger needles are used.

Twists are sometimes combined with cables, with the shallower twists complementing the depths of the cables. The advantage of twist stitches is that they can be worked more quickly than cable stitches.

Although twists are easy to do, there are lots of tiny but important variations that change the appearance of a twist. They can be worked on right- or wrong-side rows, and the stitches can be all knit, all purl or a combination of the two.

Twist stitch patterns are easy to work in the round from a chart, especially patterns that move a stitch on every row. Simply read every row of the chart from right to left, interpreting all the symbols as right-side row twists.

SEE ALSO
- **Texture and pattern, page 148**
- **Twist stitch patterns, pages 84–91**

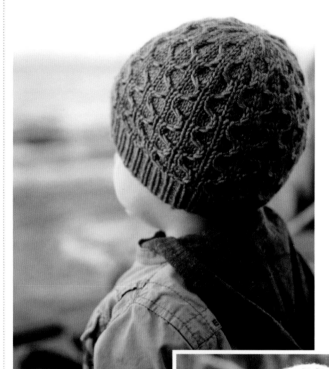

◀ **TIN CAN KNITS**
LIGHT AND SHADOW HAT
Curving lines of single stitches create a delicate interlocking pattern of light and shadow on this textured hat. This type of stitch pattern can be created using a cable needle but can also be worked quickly using twist stitch techniques.

▶ **TIN CAN KNITS**
SITKA SPRUCE BEANIE
This slouchie beanie hat is made using a twist stitch pattern to create an elegant, geometrical design inspired by the evergreen spruce trees of the rainforests of the Pacific Northwest.

Working a left twist

In this right-side row twist, the first stitch on the left needle lies on top and slants to the left, while the second stitch lies behind and is worked first through the back of the loop.

1 Knit into the back of the second stitch.

2 Knit into the front of the first stitch.

3 Slip both stitches off the left needle together.

> **LEFT TWIST VARIATIONS**
> To work a knit and purl two-stitch twist slanting to the left, purl into the back of the second stitch, then knit into the front of the first stitch.
>
> To twist two stitches to the left on a wrong-side row, purl into the back of the second stitch, then purl into the front of the first stitch.

Working a right twist

In this right-side row twist, the second stitch on the left needle lies on top and slants to the right, while the first stitch lies behind and is worked through the back of the loop.

1 Knit into the front of the second stitch.

2 Knit into the back of the first stitch.

3 Slip both stitches off the left needle together.

> **RIGHT TWIST VARIATIONS**
> There are two other ways of working the knit twist shown above. Either knit into the front instead of the back of the first stitch in step 2; or knit two together, then knit the first stitch again before slipping the stitches off the left needle.
>
> To work a knit and purl right twist, knit into the front of the second stitch, then purl into the front the first stitch.
>
> To twist two stitches to the right on a wrong-side row, purl into the front of the second stitch, then purl into the front of the first stitch.

Herringbone twist

MULTIPLE OF 6 STITCHES PLUS 3

This pattern is often used as a side panel on garments or even socks.

Tiny trellis

MULTIPLE OF 4 STITCHES PLUS 2

If worked over 10 stitches, this pattern makes a crossed diamond panel.

Miniature braid

MULTIPLE OF 4 STITCHES PLUS 1

Use this pattern as an interesting alternative to rib; simply plan more purl stitches between braids to suit your design.

Branched rib

MULTIPLE OF 16 STITCHES PLUS 2

This decorated rib does not pull in very much, so it can be used as an all-over pattern. If you want all the branches to twist in the same direction, repeat the first or last eight stitches of the chart.

Bellflower blocks

MULTIPLE OF 8 STITCHES PLUS 6

Simply twisting the stitches at the top of each block produces this pretty pattern. See the bellflower motif on page 91 for another use of these blocks.

Slip stitch ovals

MULTIPLE OF 12 STITCHES PLUS 8

Slipping stitches on wrong-side rows beneath the twist gives a graceful curve to oval mock cables.

Mock cable I

MULTIPLE OF 8 STITCHES PLUS 1

Easier than it looks, this attractive pattern uses three-stitch twists.

Mock cable II

MULTIPLE OF 5 STITCHES PLUS 2

Simple twist stitches on the right side and purl rows on the wrong side make an easy stitch with plenty of texture.

Twisted rib

MULTIPLE OF 4 STITCHES PLUS 2

(WS) P into front of 2nd st on left needle, p into first st, sl both sts off needle tog.

Twisting together two stitches on every row makes a firm, well-defined rib.

Two-twist lattice

MULTIPLE OF 8 STITCHES PLUS 2

For a three-twist lattice, simply work rows 1 and 2 twice, then rows 3 to 10. Work rows 11 and 12 twice, then rows 13 to 20, making a 24-row repeat.

For a wider lattice, work on a multiple of 10 stitches, allowing two more purl stitches between twists on the first row, then moving the stitches four times to create the diamond shapes.

Slip stitch lattice

MULTIPLE OF 14 STITCHES PLUS 2

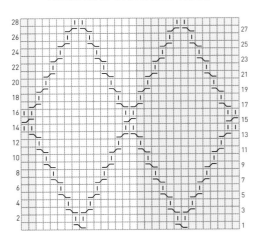

Slipping the travelling stitches on wrong-side rows makes them lie smoothly, and because they are stretched over two rows, they can be seen clearly even though the background is stocking stitch.

Zigzags

MULTIPLE OF 12 STITCHES

Stocking stitch zigzags are outlined with twisted stitches for more definition and surface texture.

Inverted pyramids

PANEL OF 26 STITCHES

The twisted stitches inside the inverted pyramids could be cabled, but twisting them gives a smoother texture.

Slip stitch diagonals

MULTIPLE OF 16 STITCHES PLUS 7

Slipping the travelling stitches on the previous row elongates and gives extra definition to these diagonals and ribs.

Wave and twist

MULTIPLE OF 14 STITCHES PLUS 2

Twist stitches are good for giving the effect of Aran knitting in miniature.

Twist stitch band

MULTIPLE OF 4 STITCHES PLUS 7

This band appears to sit on the surface of the knitting because of the increases in the first row and the decreases that are made in the last row.

▼   Increase 2 sts by working [k1, yo, k1] in st.

△   Decrease 2 sts by working ssk, then sl rem st back on to left needle and pass 2nd st on needle over.

Skeleton leaf

MOTIF OF 23 STITCHES

Slipped travelling stitches make a skeleton leaf pattern against a subtle knit and purl textured shape.

Branching leaves

PANEL OF 27 STITCHES

You will find this 20-row repeat quite easy to follow, even though you do need to watch out for twists on the wrong-side rows.

Bellflower motif

MOTIF OF 28 STITCHES

Since you cannot really knit stitches horizontally, you will need to embroider two chain stitches to complete the curve at the top of the stem when you have finished knitting. The rest of the motif is surprisingly simple.

Lace

Lace stitch patterns are simply a combination of decreases and open increases. The new stitches are made by taking the yarn over the needle, creating a light and airy effect.

The easiest lace patterns have each increase worked next to the corresponding decrease, so the stitch count stays the same on every row. In other patterns, the increases and decreases occur at different places along the row, but you will find these just as easy to work because the total number of stitches on each row does not change. For some beautiful laces, the increases and decreases are made on different rows, making it harder to keep track of the stitch count, but creating exquisite patterns.

The choice of yarn affects the appearance of lace knitting. Firm, smooth yarns make the design more visible; soft or brushed yarns blur the pattern. Traditionally, very fine wool or cotton is worked on relatively large needles. When the work is pinned and blocked, the delicate texture of the lace is revealed.

SEE ALSO
• **Design and inspiration, pages 134–155**
• **Lace stitch patterns, pages 94–101**

Making a yarn over

It is essential to take the yarn over the needle so that the strand lies in the same direction as the other stitches. Working into this strand on the next row makes a hole, but if the strand is twisted, the hole will close up. When the stitch before a yarn over is purl, the yarn will already be at the front, ready to go over the needle.

To make a yarn over between two knit stitches, bring the yarn to the front as if to purl, then take it over the needle to knit the next stitch.

To make a yarn over between a knit and a purl stitch, bring the yarn to the front as if to purl, then take it over the needle and bring it to the front again, ready to purl.

◄ FIONA MORRIS
PEWTER CARDIGAN

This cardigan uses two versions of the same lace pattern, one in stocking stitch (on the main body) and one using knit and purl stitches (at the hem, inset). The lace pattern uses a large double yarn over eyelet and the edges of the cardigan are finished with garter stitch.

Making multiple yarn overs

Some lace patterns have larger holes made by working two or more yarn overs together. The extra yarn overs may be dropped on the following row, so that only one stitch is increased, or they may all be worked so that several stitches are made.

Bring the yarn to the front, then take it over the needle. Repeat this process for each of the remaining yarn overs, then work the next stitch.

Simple all-over faggot lace
A very open-mesh texture is made over an even number of stitches by working yarn over, knit two stitches together along every row.

Creating lace patterns

Designing a lace stitch pattern is easier than it may seem. Start by looking at the charted examples in this book. In order to prevent the knitted fabric from getting progressively wider by the addition of yarn overs, there needs to be an equal number of decreased stitches. Each row does not have to end with the same number of stitches, but the number of stitches at the start of the stitch pattern repeat and at the end should be the same. The distance between a decrease and a yarn over is also an important factor in lace design – placing them next to each other or spaced apart will create different effects. In addition, working increases and decreases only on right-side rows creates a different effect from patterning on every row.

When you are ready to start designing, begin by charting the position of the yarn overs and the areas of more solid knitting, then position the decreases. However, as with all knit design, the only way to understand the fabric you are creating is to knit a swatch.

Decreases next to yarn overs
The decreases are worked immediately to one side of the yarn overs and add sharp definition to the zigzag.

Decreases and yarn overs spaced apart
The decreases are worked a few stitches away from the yarn overs and so create gently wandering lines up the fabric.

Decreases and yarn overs on every row
The patterning is on every row, giving a lacier appearance as well as a less sharply angled chevron.

Decreases and yarn overs on alternate rows
The steep angle of these chevrons is the result of patterning on alternate rows.

Feather and fan

MULTIPLE OF 14 STITCHES PLUS 1

◪ K4 tog.

◤ Sl 2 knitwise, k2 tog tbl, pass sl sts over.

This is an old Shetland lace stitch pattern with many variations. Common to them all is the grouping of increases and decreases separately from each other along the row to make patterns resembling feathers, fans, waves and scallops.

Cabled feather

MULTIPLE OF 19 STITCHES PLUS 2

Cables have been added to this feather and fan pattern. Some of the decreases are worked two rows away from the increases, resulting in a different stitch count in two of the rows.

Old shale

MULTIPLE OF 18 STITCHES PLUS 1

This version of a famous Shetland lace stitch is particularly simple and rhythmic.

Lace ladder

MULTIPLE OF 4 STITCHES PLUS 2

Very smooth and controlled, this ladder is quite stable in spite of its open texture.

Bird's eye

MULTIPLE OF 4 STITCHES PLUS 4

All-over double eyelets make an unusually textured lace pattern.

Scotch faggot cable

MULTIPLE OF 12 STITCHES PLUS 8

Cabling a faggot rib creates a stitch that can be used as an all-over repeat or in conjunction with other open stitches.

Leaves and berries

PANEL OF 21 STITCHES PLUS 2

● [K1, p1, k1, p1, k1] all into one st, making 5 sts from one, turn, p5, turn, lift 2nd, 3rd, 4th and 5th sts over first and off needle, k st tbl.

Bobbles are very compatible with many lace stitches. Here, clusters of bobbles have been added to a leaf stitch.

Tulip

PANEL OF 13 STITCHES

Many pictorial effects can be achieved with lace stitches – this tulip is slightly embossed.

Small heart I

MOTIF OF 11 STITCHES

This simple heart could be used as a repeat pattern or scattered among other motifs.

Small heart II

MOTIF OF 13 STITCHES

◿ K2 tog, return st to
left needle, pass next
st over it, sl st back
on to right needle.

This heart motif could also
be used as a leaf motif.

Pierced heart

MOTIF OF 21 STITCHES

Yarn overs and their corresponding
decreases help to shape this heart
as well as decorate it.

Picot heart

MOTIF OF 24 STITCHES

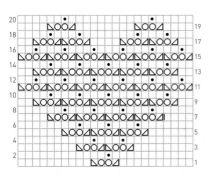

The double eyelets that make this heart
motif have a heart shape themselves, made
by working p1, k1 into the double yarn over,
instead of the usual k1, p1.

Diamond spiral

This simple but sophisticated panel would work well alongside cables.

Candlelight

Lace knitting lends itself to flame- and leaf-like patterns. In each of these motifs, the decreases move away from the increases, pulling the stitches into outlines.

Falling leaves

This is similar to the candlelight pattern (left) in construction, but the decreases pull the stitches in to form the central vein of each leaf.

Feather lace

MULTIPLE OF 8 STITCHES PLUS 11

Here, increases outline long, feather-like shapes.

Paired leaves

PANEL OF 29 STITCHES

The increases and decreases form drooping leaves with veins and make the lower edge strongly shaped.

Clustered leaves

PANEL OF 13 STITCHES

▲ K3 tog.

Repeating all 16 rows of this chart makes an attractive panel. A single repeat makes a large motif, or one of the leaves can easily be adapted to make a tiny motif.

Gothic lace

MULTIPLE OF 8 STITCHES PLUS 1

This is a progression of the feather lace pattern on page 99. One repeat of the chart makes a border, while repeating rows 1 to 16 produces an all-over pattern.

Leaf cascade

MULTIPLE OF 16 STITCHES PLUS 17

Despite the background being very open, this is not a difficult stitch to knit, but note the use of two different double decreases.

Fern edging

CAST ON 10 STITCHES

This leafy edging in garter stitch has large eyelets made with multiple yarn overs.

--- Cast off.

✱ St remaining after casting off.

Mesh lace edging

CAST ON 14 STITCHES

This pattern is based on garter stitch, so either side can be used as the right side. This picture shows the smooth side.

--- Cast off.

✱ St remaining after casting off.

Diamond edging

CAST ON 10 STITCHES

This is a classic edging that has many uses. Careful pressing is required to open out the lace. After working rows 1 to 14, repeat only rows 3 to 14.

Bobbles, knots and leaves

Increases and decreases can be used to embellish a knitted surface with three-dimensional stitches, creating a variety of interesting effects.

A group of increased stitches, decreased abruptly, makes a knot or a bobble that can be used to add emphasis to a familiar cable or lace pattern. Bobbles, knots and leaves are often worked on a reverse stocking stitch background to emphasise the contrast.

Knots are worked into one stitch and completed without turning the work. Bobbles are also worked into one stitch but have extra rows added by turning and working the bobble stitches only. Different size bobbles can be scattered or clustered according to the design.

Both knots and bobbles are worked into a single stitch and are completed before the next stitch on the left needle is worked. Leaf designs are often constructed in the same way as bobble stitch combinations, but the stitches are worked over several rows.

There is also a family of all-over textured popcorn and blackberry stitches that are made from repeated groups of increases and decreases that alternate on following rows.

SEE ALSO
- **Basic cast-ons, pages 16–17**
- **Decreases and increases, pages 28–34**
- **Texture and pattern, page 148**
- **Bobble, knot and leaf stitch patterns, pages 104–111**

Knots and bobbles
The top line shows three-stitch knots; the three sizes of bobbles below are worked using five and seven stitches over different numbers of rows.

Party dress
Bobbles and leaves are a feature of this pretty outfit.

MAKING THE PERFECT BOBBLE
Always read the pattern instructions carefully. There are more bobbles than most designers can name or chart illustrators create unique symbols for. A familiar symbol may not represent the same process as the last time you saw it.

Knit the edge stitches firmly and adjust them with the needle tip as necessary.

In general, it is better not to work a bobble too tightly. This makes it easier to work and results in a fluffy, pleasing bobble. If the first stitch after a bobble is baggy, knit into the back of it – the twisted stitch will be hidden by the bobble.

If making a large bobble, you may find it easier to use a third needle to work the bobble – perhaps one slightly larger. Look for one with a sharp tip.

Making a three-stitch knot

Knots are always made on right-side rows.

1 Cast on three stitches by working as for a cable cast-on, but work into the front of the previous stitch rather than in the space between stitches.

2 Knit the three cast-on stitches, then knit the original stitch again, making four new stitches on the right needle.

3 To complete the knot, lift three stitches, one at a time, over the last stitch on the right needle.

Making a five-stitch bobble

Bobbles are always started on a right-side row.

1 Into a stitch, work [k1, yarn over needle] twice, then k1 again, making five stitches on the right needle.

2 Then turn and purl the five stitches. Turn and knit five stitches.

3 To complete the bobble, turn, p2 together, p1, p2 together, turn, slip 2 knitwise, k1, pass the slipped stitches over. As a variation, complete the bobble by lifting the stitches over in the same way as the three-stitch knot on the left.

Making a seven-stitch leaf

Larger groups of decorative increases and decreases worked over several rows make a blister – a flat, raised shape – or a leaf that can be used as part of a motif or be integrated into a stitch pattern. The three leaves below are the same size but each made slightly differently. In all of them, pairs of increases are followed by pairs of decreases, worked at the sides or in the centre.

Creating a leaf with a vein effect
This leaf has yarn overs each side of the centre stitch. The base of the leaf conforms easily to the fabric around it.

Creating a firmer leaf shape
Lifted-strand increases each side of the centre stitch are used to shape the base of the leaf. This type of leaf shape is raised from the fabric around it.

Creating a softer, smooth leaf shape
Seven stitches are worked into a double yarn over at the start of this leaf. This type of leaf shape is raised from the fabric around it and is malleable.

Blackberry stitch

MULTIPLE OF 4 STITCHES

Ⓥ [K1, p1, k1]
all into one st,
making 3 sts
from one.

△ P3 tog.

This all-over nubbly pattern is also
known as trinity stitch, because three
stitches are made from one and one
from three on alternate rows.

Knotted rib

MULTIPLE OF 6 STITCHES PLUS 2

◉ K into front, back
and front of st,
making 3 sts from
one, lift 2nd and
first sts over 3rd
and off needle.

Here, the very smallest possible
knot adds texture to the smooth
surface of a rib stitch worked
through the back of the loops.

Bobble rib

MULTIPLE OF 5 STITCHES PLUS 2

Ⓖ [K1, yo, k1, yo, k1]
all into one st,
making 5 sts from
one, turn, k5, turn,
p5, lift 4th, 3rd, 2nd
and first sts over 5th
and off needle.

Crunchy bobbles are worked so closely
together in this pattern that they make
the rib spread out instead of pulling in.

Bobble blocks

MULTIPLE OF 6 STITCHES PLUS 1

⑤ [K1, yo, k1, yo, k1] all into one st, making 5 sts from one, turn, k5, turn, skpo, k3 tog, lift first st over 2nd and off needle.

Purl stitch bobbles are placed in regular rows on stocking stitch blocks, and outlined in alternating knit and purl stitches.

Bobble and wave

MULTIPLE OF 8 STITCHES

⑤ [K1, yo, k1, yo, k1] all into one st, making 5 sts from one, turn, k5, turn, p5, lift 4th, 3rd, 2nd and first sts over 5th and off needle.

The wave rib is not cabled; it is made with increases and decreases. The bobbles add an accent at the curve of each wave.

Triple nosegay

MULTIPLE OF 17 STITCHES PLUS 1

⑤ [K1, yo, k1, yo, k1] all into one st, making 5 sts from one, turn, k5, turn, p5, lift 4th, 3rd, 2nd and first sts over 5th and off needle.

The traditional nosegay pattern has just two branches with four bobbles. Work through the chart a few times, and you may see how to make a nosegay pattern with even more branches.

Wave and knots cable

MULTIPLE OF 8 STITCHES

◎ K into front and back of st twice, making 4 sts from one, lift 3rd, 2nd and first sts over 4th and off needle.

Knots are faster to work than bobbles because you do not have to turn the work. You could substitute the large knot shown here with any of the smaller bobbles from other designs.

Three-bobble cable

MULTIPLE OF 10 STITCHES PLUS 1

◎ [K1, yo, k1, yo, k1] all into one st, making 5 sts from one, turn, k5, turn, p5, lift 4th, 3rd, 2nd and first sts over 5th and off needle.

Cabled ovals enclose three crunchy, purl stitch bobbles. The large cable cross uses five stitches (an odd number) to give a centre stitch on which to position the bobbles.

Strawberry bobble

MULTIPLE OF 12 STITCHES PLUS 1

◎ [K1, yo, k1] all into one st, making 3 sts from one, turn, k3, turn, p3, lift 2nd and first sts over 3rd and off needle.

Bobbles can be used as an accent on lace stitches as well as cables. The berry motifs are arranged as a half-drop pattern here, but it would be easy to make a panel by repeating just the first 12 rows.

Large leaf and twists

MULTIPLE OF 26 STITCHES PLUS 1

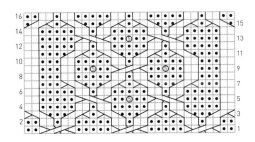

Sl 1 purlwise, k1,
yo, k1, lift sl st over
the k1, yo, k1 and
off needle.

The little twists at each side of the leaf are very simple,
but as the leaf expands and contracts it curves the twists,
making the pattern look more complicated than it really is.

Bobble and braid cable

PANEL OF 29 STITCHES

⊚ [K1, yo, k1, yo, k1] all into one st, making
5 sts from one, turn, k5, turn, p5, lift 4th, 3rd,
2nd and first sts over 5th and off needle.

This cable panel uses a five-stitch cross, so there
is a centre stitch on which to place the bobble.

Heart leaf

MOTIF OF 11 STITCHES

⬆ [Sl 1 knitwise] twice, [sl 1 purlwise, lift 1 st over and off right needle, sl st back on to left needle, lift 1 st over and off left needle] twice, p st that remains.

The surface of this motif is only slightly raised because most of the increases have compensating decreases.

Bell pattern

MULTIPLE OF 4 STITCHES PLUS 4

Ω   Cast on 1 st using backward loop cast-on method, twisting the loop before placing it on the needle.

To work a frilled edging from this chart, cast on a multiple of 12 stitches plus 4, then starting with the third row, k8 where the cast-on stitches are indicated. Follow the chart to make the bell shapes and you will end with a stitch count that is a multiple of four.

Puff stitch

MULTIPLE OF 10 STITCHES PLUS 2

ᒫ   Use left needle to lift strand between sts from the front, then knit into front of it to increase 1 st and make a small hole beneath.

Regular increases and decreases give a slightly raised surface to this pattern but it is easy to work because, despite making and losing stitches on each right-side row, the stitch count remains constant.

Flower sprigs

MULTIPLE OF 14 STITCHES PLUS 1

These pretty little motifs have slender leaves because the open increases are taken into the reverse stocking stitch stitch background.

⑤ [K1, yo, k1, yo, k1] all into one st, making 5 sts from one, turn, p5, turn, k5, lift 4th, 3rd, 2nd and first sts over 5th and off needle.

Cable with leaf and bobbles

PANEL OF 25 STITCHES

③ K into front, back and front of st, making 3 sts from one, turn, p3, turn, k3, lift 2nd and first sts over 3rd and off needle.

Work supplementary leaf chart each time the 1-stitch, 11-row symbol is indicated.

The leaf is given a separate chart to make it easier to follow the cable pattern.

Celtic vine

PANEL OF 21 STITCHES

Inspired by tree-of-life carvings on early stone crosses, this design has a separate small chart for the leaf to make it easier to follow the chart when working the curved, cabled stem.

Work supplementary leaf chart each time the 1-stitch, 11-row symbol is indicated.

⑤ [K1, yo, k1, yo, k1] all into one st, making 5 sts from one, turn, p5, turn, k5, turn, p2 tog, p1, p2 tog, turn, sl 2 sts as if to work k2 tog, k1, pass sl sts over.

Afterthought flower

PANEL OF 9 STITCHES AND 12 ROWS

This very adaptable motif is not quite an afterthought because you do need to plan enough moss stitch background and place the bobbles. A minimum of 7cm (3in) in moss stitch is needed all around the bobble area to place the petals. You could vary the size and number of petals to suit the scale of your yarn.

Work each marked stitch as k on RS and p on WS for the moss stitch background. When you have finished knitting the background, lift the stitch indicated and work (k1, yo, k1) into it for the first row of the supplementary petal chart. Continue working the petal, detached from the background, then fasten off and sew in place.

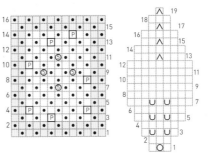

P Lift stitch and work supplementary petal chart.

5 [K1, yo, k1, yo, k1] all into one st, making 5 sts from one, turn, p5, turn, k5, lift 4th, 3rd, 2nd and first sts over 5th and off needle.

Stranded colour knitting

All around the world, people have developed traditions of colour knitting. Among the best known are patterns from Fair Isle, Scandinavia, Eastern Europe and South America.

Most stranded colour knitting is worked in stocking stitch with just two colours in a row. One or both of these colours may be changed on subsequent rows. Some patterns use three or even four colours in a row, but this can make the fabric very thick.

Stranded colour knitting is usually worked from a chart. Read the chart as directed, count the squares and work the stitches in the first colour and second colour along the first row. Once you have established the first row, you can simply glance at the chart to see how the motifs change.

In many traditions, stranded colour knitting is worked in the round, making it easy to see the pattern. If you are colour knitting in the round, read each row of the chart from right to left. As you will discover, most traditional Fair Isle patterns change colour after no more than seven stitches in a row, with the yarn not in use stranded loosely on the wrong side of the work. Stranding across more stitches would make an over-long strand, so it is best if the yarn not in use is woven in at regular intervals to keep the wrong side tidy.

◀▼ LUISE ROBERTS
FAIR ISLE THROW
A knitted Fair Isle tube has been attached along one edge of a plain length of cloth to make a stylish throw. The use of a tube conceals the reverse-side stranding of the Fair Isle and makes the finished throw double-sided. The tube is first folded flat and edged with a round of double crochet, then sewn to the cloth using whip stitch.

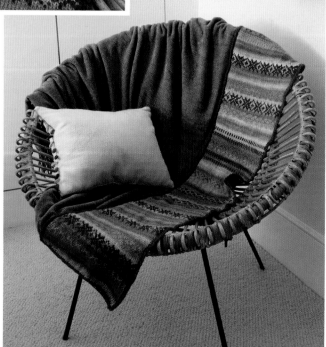

FAIR ISLE PATTERNS
The northern coast of Scotland has a strong tradition of colour knitting referred to as Fair Isle. The rich use of colour often makes stitch patterns appear very intricate, but they usually have short repeats and use only two colours in each row. One yarn is often described as the background yarn and the other as the motif yarn, and each may be changed every row or few rows.

SEE ALSO
• **Colour in design, pages 144–147**
• **Stranded colour stitch patterns, pages 114–121**

Holding the yarns

The simplest way to change colours is to drop one yarn and pick up the other. However, for faster knitting, experiment with the following techniques.

Yarns

Using a variegated yarn can produce the visual richness of frequent colour changes, but without all the yarn ends you would get from using several single-colour balls of yarn.

Holding one yarn in each hand

Wrap one yarn around each first finger from front to back. To knit and purl, work each yarn in your preferred way (see pages 14–15). For purl stitches, always move the required yarn to the front, work the stitches and move the yarn to the back before moving or working the other yarn.

Holding both yarns in the left hand

Wrap both yarns around your first finger from front to back. To knit, insert the right needle into the next stitch and select the yarn as required – always going either to the left or the right of the front yarn to reach the yarn behind. For purl stitches, take care not to twist the yarns – you may find it easier to slip a yarn that is not being worked over the middle finger.

Holding both yarns in the right hand

Wrap one yarn around your first finger and the other around the middle finger from front to back. Knit the yarn over the first finger in the usual way and knit yarn over the middle finger by turning the hand slightly to flick the yarn from the finger. For purl stitches, you may find it easier to manipulate the yarn from the first finger between thumb and first finger, and hold the yarn from the middle finger over the first finger.

Working with more than one yarn

Although this style of knitting involves working with more than one yarn, only one yarn is actually knitted at any one time – the other is looped or carried across the wrong side of the work until it is next required. Depending on the stitch pattern, the yarn not in use can be carried along the row by stranding or weaving the yarn on the wrong side of the work.

Stranding

If the yarn is not going to be in use for only a few stitches, then stranding is the best option. The strands carried across should be tensioned loosely and evenly so that the knitting lies flat. Decide which colour will lie on top and always strand the yarns in the same order.

Weaving

If the yarn is not going to be in use for more than five to seven stitches, then weaving is the best option. The yarn not in use is woven over and under, making a very firm fabric. Take care that the contrast colour does not show through to the right side.

TWISTING THE YARNS

An alternative to stranding or weaving is to twist the yarns around each other; see how to link colour areas on page 123.

Peerie patterns

Little two- and three-row patterns like these are often used as a contrast between more complex bands of motifs. However, they can also be used as all-over stitch patterns. Have fun varying the colours on a striped or plain background for an easy-to-knit version of classic Fair Isle.

MULTIPLE OF 8 STS PLUS 1

MULTIPLE OF 4 STS PLUS 1

MULTIPLE OF 4 STS PLUS 1

MULTIPLE OF 8 STS PLUS 1

MULTIPLE OF 4 STS PLUS 1

MULTIPLE OF 8 STS PLUS 1

Flower borders

Some of these small borders are built up out of peerie patterns, while others stand alone. Here, the background is all one shade, but for a more authentic colour scheme, change the background for each band of pattern.

MULTIPLE OF 20 STS PLUS 1

MULTIPLE OF 20 STS PLUS 1

MULTIPLE OF 12 STS PLUS 1

MULTIPLE OF 8 STS PLUS 1

Starflower with diamond flower border

MULTIPLE OF 20 STITCHES PLUS 1

Instead of gently shading the colours of either the background or motif yarns, here the colour changes in the motif and background are made on the same row. This adds to the jazzy feel of this bright interpretation of a traditional star with peerie patterns.

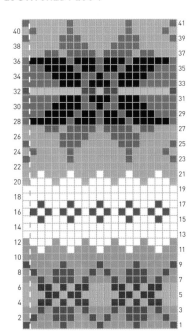

Armada crosses

MULTIPLE OF 24 STITCHES PLUS 1

The first band of pattern shows a simple version of the cross; the second is more complex. Both of these are variations on X and O patterns. For an all-over pattern, continue travelling the double line of yellow stitches over the navy background on rows 12, 13 and 14, then on rows 34, 35 and 36 to join up the X motifs.

Scandinavian stripes

MULTIPLE OF 4 STITCHES PLUS 1

Worked in monochrome —
black and white, or brown
and natural — these
versatile patterns are
typically Scandinavian,
but if you shade the
background, they will
look like Fair Isle. Similar
patterns in solid, bright
colours can be found on
Turkish socks.

Snowflake border and flea pattern

MULTIPLE OF 24 STITCHES PLUS 1

The flea pattern at the top of this sample
is a simple seeding pattern that can be
varied with many different spacings,
depending on the repeat of the pattern it
is worked with. If you want to work the
pretty Norwegian snowflake as an all-
over pattern, simply repeat rows 9 to 32.

Rosebuds and ivy

MULTIPLE OF 10 STITCHES PLUS 1

These very pretty patterns are inspired by Swedish mittens. Work rows 17 to 26 for just one row of rosebuds, or repeat rows 17 to 38 for an all-over pattern.

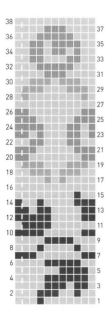

Harebells and vine

MULTIPLE OF 12 STITCHES PLUS 1

The vine borders are shown running in opposite directions. If you want to knit the next band of harebells with the flowers facing right, read rows 9 to 31 in the opposite direction.

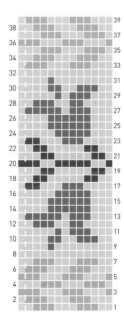

Roses and vine

MULTIPLE OF 12 STITCHES

To space the rose motif as in the swatch, begin each subsequent repeat of the 9th row five stitches in from the right of the chart. Work the 10-row rose motif twelve times before the pattern repeats exactly on row 121.

Latvian morning stars

MULTIPLE OF 16 STITCHES PLUS 1

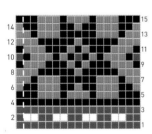

Use this striking star as a border or arrange it as a half-drop all-over pattern, as shown above.

Large reindeer

MULTIPLE OF 30 STITCHES PLUS 1

Although most of this pattern has been designed for stranded knitting, you may find it easier to use separate balls of yarn for some sections of the design.

Latvian stars

MULTIPLE OF 18 STITCHES PLUS 1

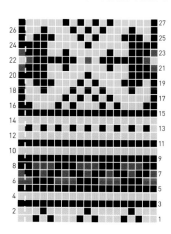

A series of stacked, geometric border patterns contrasting with an all-over design are typical of the patterns found on Latvian mittens. This design is quite easy to knit, because only row 22 has more than two colours.

Turkish sock pattern

MULTIPLE OF 12 STITCHES PLUS 1

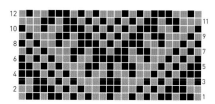

Each side of the centre stitch is a mirror image of the other, and the multiple of 12 stitches is counted each side of the centre stitch. Here, the background colour is changed every six rows, but you could use just one colour or change the background as often as you wish.

Turkish arrowhead

MULTIPLE OF 6 STITCHES PLUS 1

This pattern is easy to knit, but capable of subtle variation. Try reversing the direction of the motif on a striped background.

Star with shaded waves

MULTIPLE OF 12 STITCHES PLUS 1

This little star shows how the tone of the colours you use can emphasise the motif. When choosing colours to work this motif, make sure that you substitute your darkest shade for the brown, moving through to the lightest shade for the warm white.

Geometric patterns

These geometric designs originate from South America. The large lightning pattern is based on an embroidery design. If you would like to work a brighter version of this pattern, try working each lightning and key motif in a different colour. The smaller paddle and scroll motifs are similar to popular designs used in weaving.

MULTIPLE OF 29 STITCHES PLUS 1

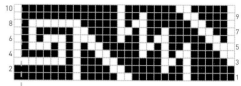

MULTIPLE OF 10 STS PLUS 1

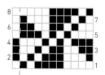

MULTIPLE OF 14 STS PLUS 1

Sawtooth border

MULTIPLE OF 5 STITCHES PLUS 1

Motifs similar to this South American geometric repeat can be found on pottery and basketwork, as well as knitting. They are often used in the same way as peerie patterns in a Fair Isle.

South American waves

MULTIPLE OF 8 STITCHES PLUS 1

Use this simple geometric pattern to move from one area of solid colour to another.

Peruvian leaf border

MULTIPLE OF 13 STITCHES PLUS 2

Strand the yarns for the purple background and pink leaf motifs, but use separate short lengths of contrasting colour for each diagonal leaf vein. Change the contrasting colour as often as you like.

Peruvian flower border

MULTIPLE OF 26 STITCHES PLUS 1

You will need to strand three colours when working this design: pink, navy and green. Just loop the green over a strand to carry it across the large gaps. The purple and yellow petals are best knitted with separate lengths of yarn. This design is very graphic and would also work well in two colours.

Intarsia colour knitting

Large geometric patterns, individual motifs and picture knits are the kind of colour designs that are best knitted using the intarsia technique.

Intarsia is simply working areas of colour with separate balls of yarn that are linked together at each colour change. This eliminates stranding or weaving in on the wrong side, and gives a single-thickness fabric. The technique is used for flat knitting only — intarsia cannot be worked in the round.

Designs in intarsia are worked from charts where the number of stitches in each colour can be seen clearly and easily. Stocking stitch is the most frequently used stitch, but the technique works just as well with textured stitches such as bobbles, cables and twists.

Some designs — such as tiny blocks of colour scattered on a plain background — are best worked in a combination of intarsia and stranding. Use separate lengths of yarn for small motifs, and strand the background colour, twisting the yarns at each colour change.

SEE ALSO
- Embroidery, page 49
- Colour in design, pages 144–147
- Stranded colour knitting, pages 112–113
- Intarsia stitch patterns, pages 124–131

TIP
Reusable peel-off stickers are ideal for keeping your place in a chart. Position them above the row you are working, so that you can see how it relates to the pattern already knitted.

◀ ZOE POWELL
BLUE MERMAID JUMPER
This jumper features sweeping bands of plain and intarsia knitting that curve around the body at different angles. The intarsia design mimics the scales on a mermaid's tail in graduating shades of blue – ideal for making use of a yarn stash.

Organising the yarns

First, sort out the yarns by counting the number of areas in each colour, then wind off suitable lengths of yarn according to the size of the areas. Use complete balls of yarn for each large area. Wind the yarn on to bobbins for smaller areas or, if there are just a few contrast stitches, use a short length of yarn.

If the design is very complex with lots of colours, avoid tangles by using lengths of yarn that can be pulled free easily because they are not attached to a ball or bobbin.

Yarn quantities

To calculate how much yarn you should wind on to a bobbin, use the chart to count the number of stitches to be worked with that length of yarn. Wrap some yarn around one of the working needles ten times; this will be enough to work ten stitches. Measure it and use this figure to calculate how much yarn you will need to complete each section of the motif. Always allow about 15cm (6in) for the yarn ends and a bit extra – just in case.

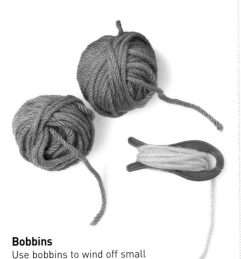

Bobbins

Use bobbins to wind off small quantities of yarn. You can buy bobbins or make your own. Alternatively, wind off small amounts of yarn into balls.

How to link colour areas

Every time you change colours, you must link the areas together or there will be holes in your knitting. All you need to do is twist the yarns on the wrong side.

On a knit row

Knit with the first colour (here, it is pink) to the changeover, then drop the yarn. Pick up the second colour (purple) and take it around the first yarn before knitting the next stitch.

On a purl row

Purl with the second yarn to the changeover. Make sure that you take the first yarn around the second yarn before knitting the next stitch.

Diagonal colour changes

It is easy to keep the knitting neat when working diagonals, because the colours move along one stitch each time and therefore linking the yarns at the changeover comes naturally. For very small areas of only a few stitches, it is sometimes easier to use duplicate stitch embroidery.

Vertical colour changes

When the colours change at the same place on several rows, be particularly careful to twist the yarns neatly and evenly to avoid holes and loose stitches. Go back at the end of the row and, using the the tip of a needle, ease any extra yarn from loose stitches towards the stitches just worked. Weave in ends along the line of colour changes and duplicate stitch any tight stitches.

Broken stripes I

MOTIF OF 29 STITCHES

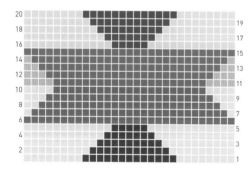

One of the simplest exercises in intarsia is to use a few diagonal colour changes to make motifs within stripes. Try light-on-dark or dark-on-light tonal variations. This motif uses darker tones on a background of lighter stripes.

Broken stripes II

MOTIF OF 29 STITCHES

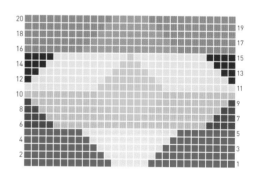

This motif uses lighter tones on a background of darker stripes.

Diamonds

MULTIPLE OF 10 STITCHES PLUS 1

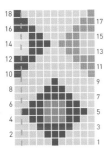

Simple geometric shapes are made more interesting by varying the colours. Instead of being carried along the row horizontally, the colours of the diamonds move diagonally up the design. The colour of the square in the centre of each diamond changes, and the background is a shaded, brushed mohair yarn.

Spots

MULTIPLE OF 16 STITCHES

Note how the chart image must be elongated to compensate for the proportions of the stocking stitch.

Sprigs

MULTIPLE OF 14 STITCHES PLUS 7

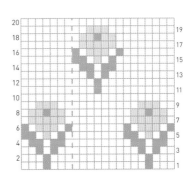

Even tiny patterns are better worked by the intarsia technique, so that there is no stranding and therefore no double thickness of fabric behind the main background colour.

Argyll checks I

MULTIPLE OF 16 STITCHES PLUS 1

Checks and plaids, such as this
pattern, are a classic way to
use blocks of colour. To keep
the number of individual lengths
of yarn to a minimum, the
overchecks can be worked in
duplicate stitch embroidery.

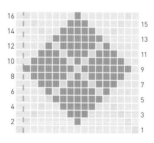

Argyll checks II

MULTIPLE OF 16 STITCHES PLUS 1

The width of the diamonds in this
design and the design to the left
are the same – they are both 15
stitches wide – but here the width
of the diamonds is increased and
then reduced by two stitches on
every second row worked. In the
design on the left, the width of the
diamonds is increased and then
reduced by two stitches on each
row worked.

Bugs

These stylised insects are made more lively with a central stripe of a deeper colour. Use one or all of them as a repeat pattern or as individual motifs.

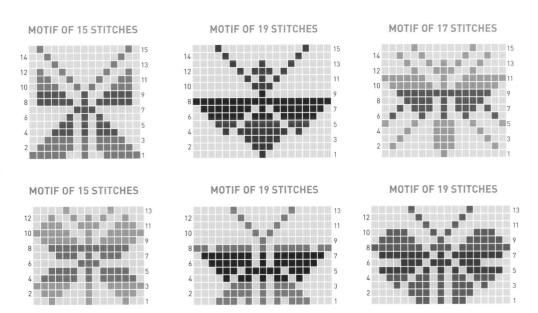

MOTIF OF 15 STITCHES

MOTIF OF 19 STITCHES

MOTIF OF 17 STITCHES

MOTIF OF 15 STITCHES

MOTIF OF 19 STITCHES

MOTIF OF 19 STITCHES

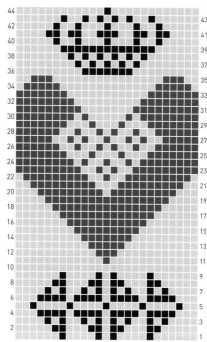

Scandinavian heart

MOTIF OF 25 STITCHES

Danish cross stitch was the inspiration
for this crowned heart motif.

Daisy border

MULTIPLE OF 12 STITCHES PLUS 1

This bright
border design
has a clear
affinity with Fair
Isle knitting, but
instead of being
the same colour
along the row,
the daisies are
each in a
different colour.

South American bird

Based on a piece of Guatemalan weaving, this mixture of intarsia and stranded colour knitting has a go-as-you-please border. The geometric repeat pattern avoids being too mechanical by having random colour changes.

MOTIF OF 39 STITCHES

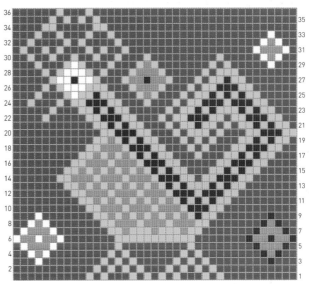

MULTIPLE OF 20 STITCHES PLUS 1

Chestnut leaves

MOTIF OF 35 STITCHES

Organic shapes inspired by nature can be particularly successful, because any slight variance from the image that inspired you can be classed as one of nature's imperfections.

Oak leaf

MOTIF OF 20 STITCHES

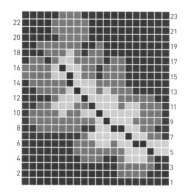

Almost any pictorial image can be knitted. The chart looks taller than the motif because of the tension.

Floral vine

MULTIPLE OF 57 STITCHES

The flower head in this elaborate
border design can be varied in
colour with each pattern repeat.

Design and Inspiration

Creating a design is simply a matter of common sense, a few calculations – and your imagination. The way in which you approach the design process will depend to a large extent on personal preference, and it may even vary from project to project. Sometimes it may start with an idea for a particular garment, while at other times it may start with a swatch you have created.

This chapter provides some practical advice on how to approach a variety of design tasks, and features a range of knitted garments, accessories and homewares to inspire you.

◀ MELANIE PORTER
HUGO GIANT KNIT BLANKET AND CUSHIONS WITH DOT LAMPSHADES
The nubbly texture of blackberry stitch is used to make these richly textured furnishings. The blanket and cushions are made using giant needles and a jumbo handspun merino yarn that is wonderfully soft and cosy. The hanging light fitting is covered with knitted lampshades made using standard-size needles and yarn.

How to Design

The secret of a good design is careful planning. It does not matter if the project is big or small, a blanket or a pair of bootees – the first step is to draw a sketch of what you would like to make. It is surprising how often this will quickly change, but it is always useful to be reminded of your starting point.

Once you are happy with a sketch, look at the drawing and think about the construction of the project. It is useful to draw a diagram or design plan of each piece that will need to be knitted, noting the direction of work and any key measurements. If the project is an item of clothing, the easiest way to ensure that you will achieve the required fit is to measure an existing garment. All measurements made on knitted fabric should be taken with the tape measure held straight along rows or stitches – never around curves. Measure from seam to seam or side to side. Of course, you can also simply take your body measurements and add ease or movement room to suit the style of your design.

Once you have a clear idea of what you would like to make, it is often useful to look through books and magazines, looking not only for similar projects but also details such as buttonbands that you like. Collect all the information together and fill in the detail in your design. Look through the following pages for more tips and advice.

TIP

After you have drawn an initial sketch, sometimes it is easier, and simpler, to find an existing pattern and adapt it to suit your needs. This could be something as simple as embellishing with beads or embroidery.

◀ TIN CAN KNITS
PRISM HAT, UNDERTONE COWL & CHROMATIC JUMPER
Don't be afraid to experiment with colour and pattern combinations. This stranded colourwork hat features a triangle motif and the jumper is a striped lace pattern, but by working both in graphic black and white they look like they were designed as a matching set (see page 146 for a colourful version of the jumper). The garter stitch cowl adds colour to the outfit and continues the stripe theme, with lines of neutral-coloured slip stitches adding vertical accents. The hot pink pompom is the delightfully fluffy cherry on top.

SEE ALSO
• Sweater design plan, pages 136–137
• Colour in design, pages 144–147

◀ **JANE SLICER-SMITH**
COCO SLUB JACKET

The basic design element of this jacket is a mitre square – rows of garter stitch with a decrease at the centre. Here they are worked into diamonds to allow the creation of the A-line styling, decreasing both stitches and needle size per mitre to achieve a tailored fit over the shoulders. Narrow stripes on each diamond accentuate the angles on the repeating mitres. The jacket is knitted in graduating shades of blue to create an ombré effect.

▼ **LYNNE WATTERSON**
FAIR ISLE THROW

Knitting a whole Fair Isle blanket may seem like a daunting task, but a deep Fair Isle panel makes an attractive addition to a fabric throw, knitted in colours to complement the decor. A pompom trim is an easy embellishment and adds both texture and a touch of fun to the finished look.

◀ **YVONNE HARLEY**
STRIPY BOOTEES

These cute little bootees worked in colourful stripes of DK yarn are embellished with knit and crochet butterflies and ladybirds finished with embroidery details. Adding your own sew-on embellishments is an easy way of personalising a design.

Sweater Design Plan

When creating a design plan for a sweater, there are several key measurements that you will need to have. The most important measurements are the width and length. Use the diagram below as a guide to the measurements required.

Sleeves and armholes

The diagram shows only half of the sleeve, so the top edge and cuff edge measurements must be doubled when calculating the width of the sleeve. For a fitted style or a shaped armhole, also record the depth and width of the armhole shaping. There is no need to draw both sleeves unless the sweater is asymmetric and has two different sleeve shapes.

Necklines

The neckline is crucial in sweaters because the sweater must fit over the head. This is particularly important when designing for young children — their head to body ratio is quite high. A neckline that is too wide can usually be fixed with an edging.

Practise good design

It is a good idea to record your design idea by making scale drawings on graph paper. This makes it easier to visualise the final design and will highlight any other measurements that still need to be resolved. It will also be useful if you are calculating the shape of a sleeve top in relation to the depth of an armhole, because the number of stitches and rows in the corresponding edges may vary and must be calculated separately. If you are working out unfamiliar shapings, you could make a full-size paper pattern or a toile before you think about calculating stitches and rows.

SEE ALSO
- **How to design, pages 134–135**
- **Calculating stitches and rows, pages 154–155**

SEE ALSO
- How to design, pages 134–135
- Calculating stitches and rows, pages 154–155

▼ **GENEVIEVE SWEENEY**
CLOVER HAND KNIT ENGINEERED RIB JUMPER
This jumper knitted in a wool and alpaca blend yarn features an all-over multidirectional rib pattern but the basic shape is a simple round-neck sweater with an oversized roll neck added.

Drop-sleeve sweater
This illustration of a simple drop-sleeve sweater shows how different proportions can be used to create two sweaters measuring the same from cuff to cuff.

▲ GENEVIEVE SWEENEY
EDIN HAND INTARSIA JUMPER

The simple shape of this crew-neck
sweater worked in luxurious cashmere
provides a canvas for a geometrical
intarsia design in rich jewel tones
and soft neutrals. The jumper is
handcrafted on a knitting frame using
a traditional hand intarsia technique.

▼ TIN CAN KNITS
DOG STAR SWEATER

Inspired by the bright star of
Sirius (the Dog Star), this Fair
Isle sweater has a classic circular
yoke shape featuring three bands
of dotted and diamond motifs
separated by plain decrease
rounds. Using small motifs and
keeping the shaping to the plain
rounds is a good introduction
to colourwork designs.

Jacket Design Plan

The same basic principles apply for designing a jacket as for designing a sweater. However, there are a few additional factors that you need to consider.

Front bands or facings

Bands can either be picked up along the front edge of a front piece, or they can be worked separately and sewn to the front edge. However, the smoothest bands are those knitted together with the fronts.

For bands that are knitted with the fronts, choose a stitch pattern with a tighter vertical tension than that used for the main fabric — for example, garter stitch with a stocking stitch main fabric. Add the number of band stitches to each front, and change stitch pattern each time you work them. Mark the buttonhole positions on your chart or pattern, and work them in as you go. For V-neck shaping, decrease in the main stitch pattern next to the band stitches and work the band stitches as before.

Repeat patterns

Scattered motifs are ideal for cardigans. All you need to do is to plan the size of the back on graph paper, then mark the position of the front edges and the shape of the neck. When placing the motifs, make sure that only whole motifs are on the fronts. To avoid having a band-sized gap on the back, you can make each front exactly half the width of the back.

SEE ALSO
- Sweater design plan, pages 136–137
- Designing a motif, pages 142–143

▶ STEPHANIE SOBEY-JONES
MERINO CABLE CARDIGAN
Hand knitted using pure merino wool, each sleeve and front piece is worked horizontally as a single piece, featuring twisted cabling together with a more sculpted cable/moss section. The back combines a rib-effect stitch with a hint of the cabling that characterises the sleeves.

TIP
Buy the buttons before you make the buttonholes.

▲ JANE SLICER-SMITH
SPLIT TEXTURE JACKET

Short-row shaping creates a sloped hemline on both the front and back. This jacket is all about detail and stitches, featuring bobbles, bells, cables, Celtic crosses, moss stitch and basket stitch. The buttonband is knitted with the front of the garment, and there is a button detail on the back hem.

▲ TIN CAN KNITS
GRAMPS CARDIGAN

This shawl-collared grandpa cardigan is knitted from the top down, with lines of stitching worked as part of the yoke to mimic raglan shaping. Stitches are picked up along the edges to knit the contrast collar and buttonbands, using short-row shaping for the shawl collar. The pockets are topped with matching bands.

Circular Yoke Design

There is no need to feel daunted when designing a circular yoke. Traditional garment shapes do not have to be worked using traditional techniques or colours. Again, the same basic principles apply as for designing a sweater, with some additional factors.

Construction

A yoke garment may be worked from the neck downwards with regular increases to create the yoke. At a point just below the underarms, the yoke is divided into two arm sections and two body sections. The front and back body sections are usually joined and work continues downwards towards the hem. A yoke garment may also be worked separately from the hem and cuffs upwards, then joined and worked in one piece to the neck edge. This method is useful if the lower body has any intarsia work.

Planning decreases

There are two ways to plan a circular yoke. With narrow bands of pattern, think of the decrease rounds as concentric circles closing in towards the centre, and place the decreases on the plain knitted rows between the bands. For large motifs, imagine the yoke as wedge-shaped segments and decrease between the motifs. Space the decreases far apart at the start, then work fewer rounds between decreases to bring the yoke in as you work towards the neck.

SEE ALSO
- Sweater design plan, pages 136–137
- Designing a motif, pages 142–143

◀ **TIN CAN KNITS**
SPOTLIGHT SWEATER
The body and sleeves of this sweater are worked separately in the round from the bottom up, and then joined to work the circular yoke featuring graphic arrow motifs in bold, bright colours. The stranded colourwork motif reduces in size from shoulder to neckline along with the yoke shaping.

◄ TIN CAN KNITS
IRONHEART SWEATER

Knitted in the round from the bottom up, this circular yoke features a lace pattern of stylised botanical motifs on a purl-textured background. The tapering motifs are designed to fit perfectly around the circular yoke and echo its shape.

► TIN CAN KNITS
LUSH CARDIGAN

Inspired by floral patterns on textiles, this cardigan features a large lace motif encircling the yoke. The cardigan has an unusual construction. The yoke is knitted first as a long strip, starting with a provisional cast-on at the centre back and working the lace design outwards to right and then left. Stitches are then picked up along the top of the lace band to work the neckline, and then from the bottom of the band to work the body and sleeves.

Designing a Motif

Simple shapes and bold designs are everywhere, so if you cannot find charted designs you like, be inspired and create your own. It is useful to remember that the more complex the image, the larger the motif will need to be to reproduce the detail, and the simpler the garment shaping should be. To establish your tension, knit a swatch of part of the chart, then work out the size of the motif. Although you can use a different yarn, add more background or frame the motif with another pattern, if you start with a motif design, the size of the motif will dictate the proportions of the garment. Alternatively, you can plan a project and design a motif or series of motifs to fit the project shapes.

SEE ALSO
- Colour in design, pages 144–147
- Texture and pattern, pages 148–153
- Colour knitting, pages 112–113 & 122–123

▼ CAT THOMAS
ZIGZAG FLOWERS PINCUSHION
Flower motifs inspired by knitting patterns from the Faroe Islands and Iceland have been used here to create a pincushion, finished with picot edging, knitted leaves and a sew-on flower button.

How to design a garment with motifs
One approach is to establish a stocking stitch tension in the yarn you want to use, estimate the size you wish the motif to be and draw the motif to fit. You may have to make some adjustments to get the best design at a size you can use.

1 Draw the motifs as accurately as you can given the limitations of graph paper, which makes drawing curves difficult. As you draw, think about the techniques you will use.

ADAPTING A CROSS STITCH CHART
Keen colour knitters are often tempted to knit from cross stitch charts. They are a particularly rich source of type designs. If you decide to adapt a cross stitch chart, remember that each cross stitch on fabric is square, whereas each knitted stitch is a wide and short V shape. With the stranded colour knitting technique, you may have an almost square tension that does not distort the design too much. However, if you use the intarsia technique to knit directly from a cross stitch chart, the design will be compressed vertically.

TIP
For large motifs, consider working small areas of a particular colour using the intarsia technique and the background stranded. Smaller motifs can be worked entirely in stranded knitting.

2 Knit swatches of each design element. Adjust the shapes and experiment with colour knitting techniques until you knit a swatch that you like.

3 Once you have designed the motif, draw a full-size chart for the back of the garment, photocopy the motif several times, then cut out the motifs and move them around on the large chart until you have the desired effect.

▲ **TIN CAN KNITS**
WAVES MITTENS

These stranded colourwork mittens feature a graphic wave pattern set beneath a starry sky. The wave motif was inspired by a Japanese-style wave motif painted on the designer's bedroom wall. The starry sky is a simple Fair Isle seeding pattern.

▶ **JENNIFER TARAN**
QUEEN OF HEARTS

The heart motif is a perennial favourite. On this stranded colourwork hat, a strip of small hearts above the corrugated rib brim frame the face, while the crown is covered with an interlocking pattern of outlined hearts. The use of a variegated yarn in shades of strawberry brings the motifs to life.

Colour in Design

Colour is not something you have to invent if you wish to design; it is something you can see in the world around you. If you love multicolour knitting, you will find inspiration wherever you look.

The colour of your project may be the first thing people notice. The colour could be the pigments you choose or the light reflected from a texture. It could be the starting point for a design, or it could be inspired by a design idea.

Charting colours

This can be a useful exercise even if you are not planning a stranded or intarsia knitted project, because it helps to establish the proportions of each colour that would suit your design best. If you do not have a charted design in mind, start with a design with a small repeat so that you can see the results of your colour experiments quickly. Use coloured crayons or pens and start by using two colours in a row, as in classic stranded colour knitting, then add more colours or incorporate tiny areas of intarsia. Colour more than one repeat to see the effect of this on the colour and pattern. Changing the background colour and the pattern colour each time can produce an interesting flickering stripe. The motifs do not need to be very complicated, because even the simplest patterns come to life if you get the colours right.

Choosing yarn colours

When you choose yarn colours, do not worry too much about matching them exactly to your inspiration. It is a mistake to be obsessive about matching colours and then forget to consider the fibre content of a yarn. A colour may look too bright in the ball, but used in tiny amounts it will wake up the softer shades. Try to think in terms of warm and cool, and light and dark, as well as pigments. Mix in a few yarns with

a slight texture to break up the regularity of the surface. Start by knitting your most successful chart design or simply start to knit and change the colours whenever you like.

SEE ALSO
• **Texture and pattern, pages 148–153**
• **Designing a motif, pages 142–143**
• **Colour knitting, pages 112–113 & 122–123**

MELANIE PORTER
HARDY VINTAGE CINEMA SEATS

Vintage 1930s cinema seats on their original wrought iron frames are given a new lease of life with felted knit upholstery in bright stripes and textured patterns. The multicoloured panels feature stripes of colour running both horizontally and vertically, with cable and rib patterns running along or across the coloured stripes for additional impact.

◀ **TIN CAN KNITS**
POP BLANKET

Inspired by the bright graphics of comic books and Pop Art, and a love of polka dots in general, this blanket is ideal for using up scraps of leftover yarn. Each square is knitted separately from the centre out, and then the squares are seamed together. Techniques used include pinhole cast-on and short-row shaping. Wet blocking is essential for achieving the perfect finish.

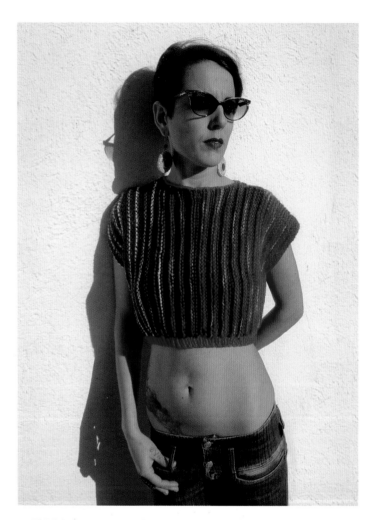

▲ ZOE POWELL
HOT TO COLD CROPTOP
This colourful top is made using a variety of stash and waste yarns, including wool, alpaca, cotton, acrylic and mix blends, with the colours carefully selected to shade from hot reds to cool blues.

▶ ALISON DUPERNEX
PIXEL THROW
This large throw is knitted in strips and then sewn together. Careful planning ensures that the correct colour is used for each square of the strips to complete the symmetrical pattern. The finished throw has been lightly felted in a washing machine.

◀ **TIN CAN KNITS**
CHROMATIC JUMPER AND BOUNCE BABY BLANKET

Simple stripes of bright colours, a lacy stitch pattern and a wide neckline combine to make a lovely summer top for a baby. The stripy blanket is a lacy shell pattern with garter stitch stripes of off-white separating the colourful shells, worked here in graduating shades of blue to create an ombré effect.

▶ MELANIE PORTER
HARRY VINTAGE 'EGG' CHAIR

This restored 1960s swivel chair is covered in a patchwork design of felted knit upholstery, with deep-set crochet buttons. The use of multiple colours and textured stitch patterns gives the chair both visual impact and tactile appeal. Compare this chair to the James chair on page 2, upholstered in monochrome neutrals, to compare how the use of colour affects the appearance of texture and pattern.

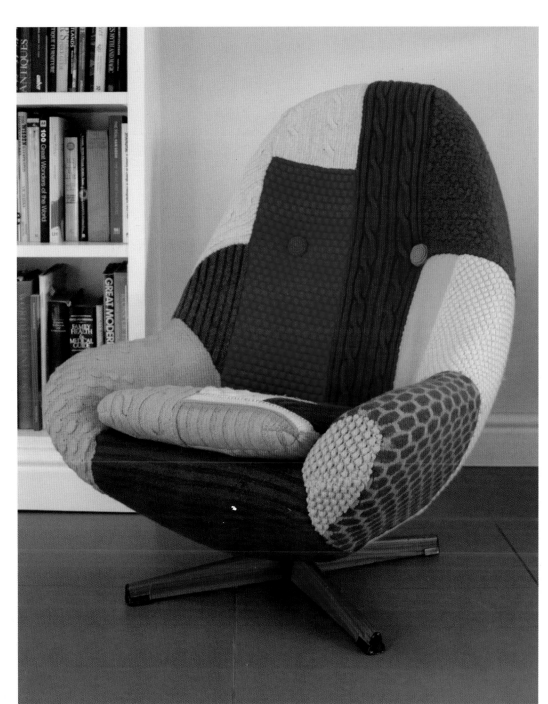

Texture and Pattern

One thing knitted fabric has in abundance is texture – it may be the simple texture of the stitch pattern, the texture of the yarn or the raised texture of bobbles and cables.

Combining textured patterns

Creating a design with textured stitch patterns is just like planning any other repeat pattern – all you have to do is use the tension to work out the measurements. The only difference is that, if you are combining cables with another stitch pattern or putting different cables together, you will need to take the tension of each cable panel and stitch pattern separately. Calculate the size of each panel, then add them together to establish the width. To adjust the design to get the measurement you want, change the number of stitches between panels. If designing a jacket or cardigan, make sure that only whole panels are on the fronts. If the back is to mirror the front pieces, make each front exactly half the width of the back to avoid having a band-sized gap on the back.

SEE ALSO
- **Colour in design, pages 144–147**
- **Calculating stitches and rows, pages 154–155**

TIP

Experiment first with a natural fibre yarn. Then, if you need to unravel a section of your knitting, you can simply steam out the crinkles by holding the yarn over a recently boiled kettle, and reuse the yarn. Rewind it very loosely.

◄▼ ELISA VANDERSCHUIT
KNITTED PLANT COVERS
Jumbo needles and yarn are combined with garter stitch and a cable pattern to make textured covers to dress up plain plant pots.

◄ JENNIFER TARAN
ZIGZAG BABY CARDIGAN
The solid-coloured zigzag lace pattern is echoed in the zigzag shape of the variegated picot edging, which helps to unify the top and bottom halves of the design and adds another layer of texture and pattern to a cute baby cardigan.

◄ ELISA VANDERSCHUIT
KNITTED THROW
The use of doubled-up
super-chunky yarn and
jumbo needles makes a
large item such as a throw
relatively quick to work up.
The basketweave stitch
pattern creates a grid of knit
and purl squares that catch
light and shadow differently,
accentuating the texture
of this rich red throw.

▲ **JEANETTE TROTMAN**
BEADED LACE SHRUG

This elegant shrug combines
an alpaca/silk blend yarn with
an openwork lace pattern. Gold
beads are knitted into the design
to complement the honey colour
of the yarn, adding another layer
of texture and enhancing the
luxurious finished look.

◄ **LYNNE WATTERSON**
HANDBAG

This elegant lined handbag
features vertical columns of cables
on a garter stitch background;
the background is interspersed
with mini-cables to create the
horizontal stripes. Clear plastic
handles and a fluffy marabou
trim add contrasting textures.

▲ MARIE CONNOLLY
FLORAL SCARF

The herringbone stitch pattern produces a textured fabric that is perfect for a cosy scarf. Knitted stems (made by casting on and then casting off a length of stitches), flower buds and bloom (made from squares of stocking stitch gathered into a ball using a line of running stitch) and a fringe of tassels add a medley of textures and colours to the neutral-coloured scarf.

▶ GENEVIEVE SWEENEY
ELKA HAND KNIT TEXTURED CABLE JUMPER

With a deep V-neck and oversized silhouette, this jumper features a textured cable pattern with links detail. It is worked on large needles using a cotton/mohair blend yarn – a chainette cotton filled with mohair fibre – to create a jumper that looks cosy and thick but is also lightweight and soft to the touch.

▶ **ELIZABETH LOVICK**
SHETLAND LACE SHAWL

This modern variation on the stole features alternating stripes of linear and circular lace patterns. It has shaped ends to add to the visual interest, with the pattern then flowing into the central section. The two tails of the shawl are worked from the shaped end and then grafted together in the middle using Kitchener stitch.

▼ **CLAIRE NEWBERRY**
CHUNKY CABLE COWL

Edged with bands of stocking stitch at top and bottom, the giant cables look like huge knit stitches running horizontally around the cowl. Although worked in two shades of cream, the contrasting smooth and fuzzy textures of the jumbo yarns – recycled jersey fabric and pure wool – set the cable pattern into high relief.

▶ **ELIZABETH LOVICK**
HEIRLOOM SHETLAND LACE BABY SET

Traditionally used for a christening, this heirloom set is ideal for any baby naming or dedication occasion. Comprising a petticoat, dress, hat and bootees, it showcases the ethereal beauty and intricacy of Shetland lace patterns. If desired, ribbons can be threaded through any of the many lines of lace holes in the dress and petticoat.

▼ **JEANETTE TROTMAN**
BUTTONED BABY BOOTEES

The moss stitch texture and cute rounded shape of these bootees are complemented by the soft cashmere blend yarn to make the perfect gift for a baby. The bootees are edged with blanket stitch and finished with a shell button.

Calculating Stitches and Rows

Once you have finished your design plan, you will need two sets of measurements to translate your design into stitches and rows – the size of your stitches and the size of your project.

First, find out the size of your stitches. To do this, write down the tension of the swatch as so many stitches and so many rows to 10cm (4in). This will be more accurate than measuring a smaller unit such as 1cm or 1in. Ensure that you have a diagram of each piece to be worked in the project, with measurements.

Number crunching

To translate the measurements into stitches and rows, use a calculator for speed and accuracy. Here, measurements are given in centimetres and inches, but always work in one or the other – do not mix them. For example, if your tension is 22 stitches to 10cm (4in), divide the stitches by 10 (4) to give 2.2 stitches per cm (5.5 stitches per inch).

To calculate how many stitches to cast on for a width of 61cm with a tension of 2.2 stitches to 1cm:
• 2.2 multiplied by 61 = 134 stitches

To calculate how many stitches to cast on for a width of 24in with a tension of 5.5 stitches to 1in:
• 5.5 multiplied by 24 = 132 stitches

Calculate the number of rows in the same way, using the row tension.

SEE ALSO
• **How to design, pages 134–135**
• **Sweater design plan, pages 136–137**

◀▲ FIONA MORRIS
MARISE TOP
This summer top is knitted in a bamboo/wool mix yarn that gives the top great drape. The stitch patterns are in fact lace patterns that look like cables. Waist shaping has been added by changing needle size rather than decreasing and increasing, and the puff sleeve uses the technique of casting off some stitches after the cuff and then casting on a larger number of stitches for the same area to work the rest of the sleeve pattern.

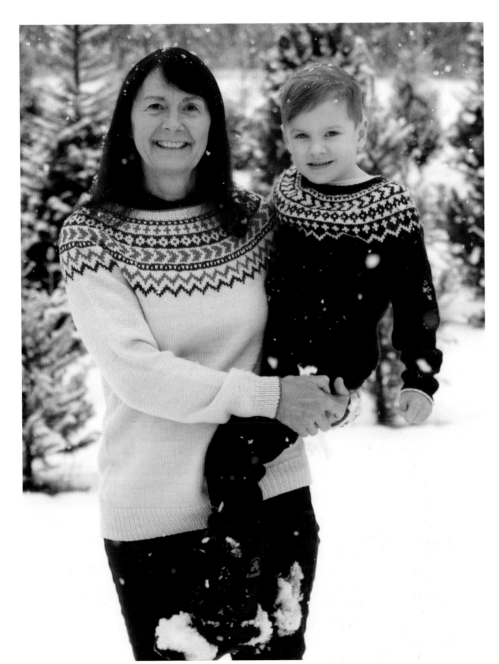

Planning repeats

If you are using stocking stitch, you can cast on the precise number of stitches needed for the width (plus two stitches that will be lost in the side seams when they are sewn up). Add or subtract a stitch or two to balance a ribbed edge. If you are using a textured stitch pattern, you will have to calculate how many multiples of the pattern – plus any edge stitches – come closest to fitting into your measurements. Check the row repeats in relation to the length in the same way.

Stocking stitch can be worked on any number of rows, but if working in a textured stitch, you may want to shape the shoulder or neck at the end of a pattern repeat or on a specific pattern row to avoid an ugly break. It is sometimes useful to draw your final design again on knitter's graph paper that matches your tension, allowing one stitch to each square. Adapt measurements or stitch patterns until you are happy with the proportions of your design. You are now as well prepared as you can be and are finally ready to start knitting the project.

◀ TIN CAN KNITS
TENDERHEART SWEATERS

Multi-sized designs require careful calculation, using test swatches, schematic drawings and graphs for planning. This Fair Isle sweater is a simple construction – each piece is worked from the bottom up and then joined for the circular yoke, featuring bands of small geometric motifs – but meticulous planning has been used to adapt the pattern for different sizes, ranging from young babies to adults.

Key to Patterns

All of the essential information that you will need for using the stitch patterns in this book is gathered here for easy reference.

Reading the charts

Each square of a chart represents one stitch, and each row represents one row of stitches.

The numbers up the sides of a chart are row numbers, and you need to progress from the bottom to the top of the chart.

All rows that are numbered on the right-hand side of a chart are read from that side and represent right-side rows. All rows that are numbered on the left-hand side of a chart are read from that side and represent wrong-side rows.

Black squares on charts are used where stitches do not exist (for example, where a stitch is lost by decreasing and is not compensated for with an increase).

Shaded areas show edge stitches or extra stitches used to balance patterns. Unshaded areas show a panel or the multiple of stitches to repeat. The number of stitches in a panel or multiple is specified for each chart, plus the extra stitches (for example, a multiple of 8 sts plus 2 means multiply 8 by the number of repeats required and then add the 2 end stitches to balance the pattern).

Sometimes stitches are outlined to make reading a chart easier – this does not affect how the stitches are worked.

Key to chart symbols

The following symbol explanations only apply if another meaning has not been indicated with the stitch pattern.

Symbol	Meaning
□	k on RS rows, p on WS rows
⊡	p on RS rows, k on WS rows
☑	k1 tbl on RS rows, p1 tbl on WS rows
■	no stitch
⊟	sl 1 wyif on RS rows, sl 1 wyib on WS rows
⊞	sl 2 wyif on RS rows, sl 2 wyib on WS rows
⊞⊞	sl 5 wyib on WS rows
Ⅱ	sl 1 wyib on RS rows, sl 1 wyif on WS rows
☒	k in front and back of stitch
Ա	lift strand between stitches and k into back of it
Ա	lift strand between stitches and p into back of it
○	yarn forwards and over needle to make a stitch
⊿	k2 tog
⊿	p2 tog
◩	sl 1 knitwise, k1, pass sl st over
◭	sl 1 knitwise, k2 tog, pass sl st over
◮	sl 2 sts as if to work k2 tog, k1, pass sl sts over
⋎⋌	sl 1 st on to cable needle and hold at back, k1, then k1 from cable needle

Symbol	Meaning
⋉⋊	sl 1 st on to cable needle and hold at front, k1, then k1 from cable needle
⋎⋌	on either RS or WS rows, sl 1 st on to cable needle and hold at back, p1, then k1 from cable
⋉⋊	on either RS or WS rows, sl 1 st on to cable needle and hold at front, p1, then k1 from cable needle
⋎⋌	sl 2 sts on to cable needle and hold at back, k1, then p2 from cable needle
⋉⋊	sl 1 st on to cable needle and hold at front, p2, then k1 from cable needle
⋎⋌	sl 1 st on to cable needle and hold at back, k2, then p1 from cable needle
⋉⋊	sl 1 st on to cable needle and hold at front, p1, then k2 from cable needle
⋎⋌	sl 2 sts on to cable needle and hold at back, k2, then k2 from cable needle
⋉⋊	sl 2 sts on to cable needle and hold at front, k2, then k2 from cable needle
⋎⋌	sl 2 sts on to cable needle and hold at back, k2, then p2 from cable needle
⋉⋊	sl 2 sts on to cable needle and hold at front, p2, then k2 from cable needle

sl 1 st on to cable needle and hold at back, k3, then p1 from cable needle

sl 3 sts on to cable needle and hold at front, p1, then k3 from cable needle

sl 3 sts on to cable needle and hold at back, k2, sl 1 st from cable needle on to left needle and p this st, k2 from cable needle

sl 3 sts on to cable needle and hold at back, k2, sl 1 st from cable needle on to left needle and k this st, k2 from cable needle

sl 2 sts on to cable needle and hold at back, k3, then p2 from cable needle

sl 3 sts on to cable needle and hold at front, p2, then k3 from cable needle

sl 3 sts on to cable needle and hold at back, k3, then k3 from cable needle

sl 3 sts on to cable needle and hold at front, k3, then k3 from cable needle

k into front of 2nd st, k into back of first st, sl both sts off left needle together

k into front of 2nd st, p into front of first st, sl both sts off left needle together

k into back of 2nd st, k into front of first st, sl both sts off left needle together

p into back of 2nd st, k into front of first st, sl both sts off left needle together

k into front of 3rd st, then 2nd st, then first st, sl 3 sts off left needle together

k into front of 3rd st, p into front of first st, then 2nd st, sl 3 sts off needle together

p into back of 3rd st, then 2nd st, k into front of first st, sl 3 sts off left needle together

Abbreviations

inc	increase/increases/increasing
k	knit
kf&b	knit into front and then back of stitch
m1	make one stitch
m1L	make one stitch slanting left
m1R	make one stitch slanting right
p	purl
pf&b	purl into front and then back of stitch
rem	remaining
rep	repeat
RS	right side
skpo	sl 1 knitwise, k1, pass sl st over
sk2po	sl 1 knitwise, k2 tog, pass sl st over
sl	slip
ssk	sl first st and then 2nd st knitwise, insert left needle into sts and k2 tog
ssp	sl first st and then 2nd st purlwise, insert left needle into sts and p2 tog
st(s)	stitch(es)
tbl	through back of loop
tog	together
WS	wrong side
wyib	with yarn in back
wyif	with yarn in front
yfwd	yarn forward
yo	yarn over
[ ]	work instructions in brackets as directed

NEEDLE SIZES

The following is only a guide. The sizes are not always exact equivalents.

Metric (mm)	American	Old UK sizes
2	0	14
2.25	1	13
2.5	–	–
2.75	2	12
3	–	11
3.25	3	10
3.5	4	–
3.75	5	9
4	6	8
4.5	7	7
5	8	6
5.5	9	5
6	10	4
6.5	10½	3
7	–	2
7.5	–	1
8	11	0
9	13	00
10	15	000

Glossary

Aran: Sweater design with cables and textured stitch patterns in natural, cream wool; originally associated with the Aran Islands, Ireland, it can now simply refer to a design with cable patterns.

Argyll: Scottish tartan sock pattern, now used to describe a diamond pattern with a superimposed plaid design.

Back (of work): The side of the work away from the knitter.

Bobbin: (i) Shape for winding on lengths of yarn, used for multicoloured knitting; (ii) wooden tube with four pegs at top, used for 4-stitch tubular knitting.

Brushed: Yarn with surface hairs raised in the manufacturing process.

Casting off: Closing stitches and removing them from needles at end of work.

Casting on: Making stitches on needle at start of work.

Chart: (i) Grid with colours or symbols representing motifs or stitch patterns; (ii) complete garment shape marked out on graph paper.

Crossed stitches: Stitches worked through the back of the loops.

Eyelets: Holes made with yarn overs and decreases; part of a lace stitch pattern.

Fair Isle: Distinctive patterns in stranded colour knitting, originally associated with the Scottish island of that name; now often used to describe many styles of multicoloured knitting.

Faggot: Lace stitch patterns using yarn overs and decreases on every row.

Front (of work): The side of the work facing the knitter.

Garter stitch: Basic stitch pattern; either knit every row or purl every row.

Gauge: (i) A device for measuring the size of knitting needles; (ii) another name for tension.

Knitwise: Inserting needle into stitch as if to knit.

Man-made yarns: Yarns from fibres made by chemical processes.

Multiple: A number of stitches grouped to form a repeat pattern along a row.

Natural fibres: Animal hair, such as alpaca, mohair or wool; plant fibre, such as cotton or linen.

Panel: A group of stitches forming a self-contained pattern.

Purlwise: Inserting needle into stitch as if to purl.

Repeat: A group of stitches or rows worked more than once to form a pattern.

Right side: The side of the stitch pattern viewed when the item is complete.

Shaping: Using increases to make the fabric wider or decreases to make the fabric narrower; these can be placed at the edges, along a row or for a dart.

Stocking stitch: Basic stitch pattern; knit on right-side rows, purl on wrong-side rows; also known as stockinette.

Tension: The number of stitches and rows to a given measurement; also known as gauge.

Turning rows (short rows): Method of shaping by working part of a row, then turning the work.

Twisted stitches: Stitches worked through the back of the loops; not to be confused with twist stitch patterns.

Wrong side: The side that will not be seen when the item is complete.

Index

Page numbers in *italic* refer to charted patterns in the stitch collection

Credits

We would like to thank and acknowledge the following for kindly supplying images of their work for inclusion in this book:

- **Alison Dupernex** pp72, 146
  www.alisondupernex.co.uk
- **Yvonne Harley** p134
  www.stichedupbyyvonne.wordpress.com
- **Fiona Morris** pp92, 154
  www.fionamorrisdesigns.co.uk
  www.distanceknitting.com
- **Claire Newberry** © 2018 p152
  www.clairenewberry.com
  Photographer: Tony Powell
  www.tonypowelldesign.co.uk
- **Melanie Porter** pp2, 132, 145, 147
  www.melanieporter.co.uk
  Photographer: Nina Duncan (p145)
- **Zoe Powell** pp122, 146
  www.zoepowell.com
- **Jane Slicer-Smith** pp135, 139
  www.sigknit.com
- **Stephanie Sobey-Jones** p138
  www.stephaniesobey-jones.co.uk
  Photographer: Claudia Hahn
  www.claudia-hahn.com
- **Genevieve Sweeney** pp136, 137, 151
  www.genevievesweeney.com
- **Jennifer Taran** pp6, 8, 143, 148
  Wool: www.fleeceandharmony.com
  Patterns by: CAWcreations (pp6, 8, 148)
  www.cawcreations.org;
  Sand and Sky Creations (p143)
  www.sandandskycreations.com
  Photographers: Amanda Stright (p6);
  Jennifer Taran (pp8, 148); Simone Van
  Iderstine (p143)
- **Tin Can Knits** pp82, 134, 137, 139, 140, 141, 143, 144, 146, 155
  www.tincanknits.com
- **Elisa Vanderschuit** pp50, 148, 149
  Song of a Sparrow Handknit Creations
  www.songofasparrow.com

The mouse on page 39 is reproduced by kind permission of *Bella* magazine.

All other photographs and illustrations are the copyright of Quarto Publishing plc. While every effort has been made to credit contributors, Quarto would like to apologise should there have been any omissions or errors – and would be pleased to make the appropriate correction for future editions of the book.

We would also like to acknowledge the work of the following authors:

- **Marie Connolly** p151
  The Very Easy Guide to Knitting Scarves
- **Elizabeth Lovick** pp152, 153
  The Magic of Shetland Lace Knitting
  Magical Shetland Lace Shawls to Knit
- **Luise Roberts** p112
  How to Knit and Crochet Blocks,
  Blankets & Throws
- **Cat Thomas** p142
  50 Pincushions to Knit & Crochet
- **Jeanette Trotman** pp33, 52, 150, 153
  Easy Beaded Knits
  Easy Knitted Accessories
  Easy Knitted Socks
- **Lynne Watterson** pp135, 150
  The Very Easy Guide to Cable Knitting
  The Very Easy Guide to Fair Isle Knitting

Thanks also to Coats Crafts UK (www.coatscrafts.co.uk) for supplying the equipment on pages 10–11 for photography, and to David Crawford for photographing the yarns on pages 12–13.